WHAT GREAT WRITI
ABOUT BABOONS

I think a proper story makes us laugh or feel sad or teaches us something important. James Dorsey tells those kinds of stories.
—Tim Cahill, cofounder of *Outside* magazine, author of
Hold the Enlightenment and *Jaguars Ripped My Flesh*

James Dorsey's writing stands out...and not just because of the remote places he visits, but because of how he views the world when he gets there, and later how he shares it with his readers. Few writers understand the story arc, how we need to start somewhere to get anywhere, and in the story, "Listening to the Silence," we witness a complete transformation. He moves from a restless, distracted trekker, to an inward looking, humbled member of the human race. From a typical tourist to a reflective man, who is, like all of us, searching, but who has found more than many have. His writing always provides not only a glimpse of the outside, but an endearing look at the inside, what he is thinking, and this adds a richness that few authors attempt.
—Max Hartshorne, editor and publisher of GoNomad.com

These stories are a reminder to us all that there is more to this world than what we see on TV news. Thank goodness! That there are welcoming and warm hearts in every corner happily willing to accommodate a wayfarer who sees them with open eyes and mind. Dorsey's Tales give us permission to be silly, soulful, and serendipitous on this adventure we call life, and a reminder of the transformative power of travel on us and on our misconceptions.
—Kimberley Lovato, travel journalist,
author of *Walnut Wine and Truffle Groves*

Whether dodging poop balls hurled by resident monkeys of a Burmese Monastery, or reflecting on the collective consciousness of mankind while visiting a shaman in Northwestern China, award-winning author James Michael Dorsey has opened his heart and mind to the cultural pulse of the societies he has encountered. *Baboons for Lunch* is a fascinating, moving, and memorable read.
—Darrin DuFord, author of *Breakfast for Alligators*
and *Is There a Hole in the Boat?*

These travel stories are big, burly, and bold—rather like James Dorsey. He also exudes humility and kindness. In *Baboons for Lunch* Dorsey masters crafting the perfect sentence and spinning an enthralling yarn. He lures us to faraway places. "At this bend of Mali's Niger River the lethargic water resembles dark roasted coffee as it slowly meanders on toward the fabled city of Timbuktu." ("Jordan's Bull")

In "From the Ashes": "The smoke of wood fires dulls the sunrise, silhouetting the spires of Angkor Wat as if in an impressionist painting, and as the sun climbs, I watch their hazy shadow retreat from my feet like an ebbing tide."

Dorsey's stories are like inviting cave mouths, yawning wide with promises of crystals, bats, and mystery, with characters both charming and eccentric. Can I resist not diving into, "Breaking Bread in Kansas": "In far Northwestern China, where a shark fin outline on a map punches Russia in the belly and divides Kazakhstan from Mongolia, invisible spirits and deities roam the land."

James Dorsey's storytelling casts a spell that is poetic, funny, and poignant. His travels take us on sweeping adventures most of us will never experience.

—Lisa Alpine, author of *Wildlife: Travel Adventures of a Worldly Woman*

A master storyteller, James Dorsey took me from one side of the world to the other with this collection of travel tales. Edgy, descriptive, hold your breath writing. Once you begin reading, this bastion of the American travel narrative will steal your afternoon. Pull up an armchair and enjoy the journey.

—Amy Gigi Alexander, explorer, writer,
publisher of *Panorama Journal*

As the editor of Perceptive Travel I've had the pleasure of publishing some of James' stories—a few appear in this book—and I always know that what he sends me won't be boring. A true explorer with more courage to face the unknown than most 20-somethings, he throws himself headlong into each situation and puts his faith in his newfound cast of local characters. With a keen eye and the patience to listen, he will continue to pile up writing awards on his memento-crowded desk back home.

— Tim Leffel, editor of *Perceptive Travel*

Ancient Societies, nomadic people: this is the travel world of cultural explorer James Dorsey. Delving into unchartered territory seems only commonplace for the curious Dorsey. The storyteller takes us to undiscovered lands, the likes of hidden regions so far from the commonplace tourist trail, excavating deep into the far regions of the Manyara Highlands that conquer western Tanzania, where he has an astounding interaction with Hadzabe Bushmen. Dorsey weaves tales of Africa that conjure up Stanley and Livingstone, interactions with delicate vanishing civilizations that few of us will ever experience. He enlightens and leaves us lingering for the serendipitous moments of travel, far from the average tale. Life lessons exquisitely told by the humanizing pilgrim author lead us down a path that involves, clans, tribes, and rare minglings, far from the human eye. The astute chronicler, Dorsey rolls the dice on life and lost societies, and has truly come out the winner.

—Nick Kontis, author of *Going Local*

When you read James Dorsey's book, *Baboons for Lunch*, be prepared to wander off the beaten path. This is a beautifully written travel memoir that explores the far reaches of the planet, from Africa to Asia, Alaska to South America, and even to mythical Timbuktu. From the humorous, to the sublime, Dorsey's prose covers the terrain of intuitive travel, and a life examined and well lived. James Dorsey is a unique and gifted writer, a nineteenth century adventurer trapped in the body of a twenty-first century writer. I suspect we haven't heard the last of James Dorsey's tales of exploration. A must read for travel enthusiasts and those who love a good Sir Richard Burton-like tale to stir the imagination.

—Tor Torkildson, series editor of *The Walkabout Chronicles*

ALSO BY JAMES MICHAEL DORSEY

Tears, Fear and Adventure
(30 Years of Travel Off the Beaten Path)

Vanishing Tales from Ancient Trails

Baboons for Lunch

And other sordid adventures

JAMES MICHAEL DORSEY

TRAVELERS' TALES
AN IMPRINT OF SOLAS HOUSE, INC.
PALO ALTO

Travelers' Tales and Solas House are trademarks of Solas House, Inc., Palo
Alto, California. travelerstales.com | solashouse.com

Cover Design: Kimberley Nelson
Cover Photograph: © James Michael Dorsey
Interior Design and Page Layout: Howie Severson
All photos by James Michael Dorsey

Library of Congress Cataloging-in-Publication Data

Names: Dorsey, James Michael, 1949- author.
Title: Baboons for lunch : and other sordid adventures : a collection of
  personal narratives / by James Michael Dorsey.
Description: Palo Alto, California : Travelers' Tales, [2018]
Identifiers: LCCN 2017052524 (print) | LCCN 2018002856 (ebook) | ISBN
  9781609521264 (ebook) | ISBN 9781609521257 (pbk.)
Subjects: LCSH: Dorsey, James Michael, 1949---Travel. | Travel--Anecdotes. |
  Travelers--Anecdotes.
Classification: LCC G465 (ebook) | LCC G465 .D67 2018 (print) | DDC
  910.4--dc23
LC record available at https://lccn.loc.gov/2017052524

Printed in the United States
10 9 8 7 6 5 4 3 2 1

This book is dedicated to my wife and best friend, Irene.
Without her, none of this would have ever happened.

Table of Contents

Author's Preface

As a young child, I preferred watching travel programs on television to playing with my friends, and each month I waited for the latest issue of *National Geographic* to take me to faraway lands.

My child's mind understood little of what I was seeing or reading, but that did not matter. They were exotic images that stirred something inside of me that I knew would take me to those places one day.

That was long before the term "adventure travel" had entered the general lexicon, because international air travel was in its infancy and the world was still recovering from a world war. Somehow, over the years, I managed to merge a talent for story telling with my lust for wandering, and joined the ranks of those known as travel writers.

Now I'm willing to concede that storytelling is most likely not the worlds' oldest profession, but I believe it to be a close second.

Most of us know what the oldest profession is generally considered to be, but I would wager the first storyteller was the fellow who just finished utilizing that profession and wanted to brag about it to his male friends.

Since none of us were present when the first story was told, we can really only speculate about its origin, but, it probably happened not long after mankind realized that making sounds gave weight to thought. If you are Christian the first story was told by Eve to Adam when she said it was okay to eat that apple. That was the beginning of fiction. For others, the first story was probably told around a fire inside a cave and might have gone something like this, "long ago and far away..."

No? Well, consider this.

You are probably thinking about that first story now and maybe even smiling, because a good story should inform and entertain while provoking thought. If you throw in "educate" you've got a very cool definition.

Fortunately for us storytellers, the Mesopotamians got tired of simply talking and conjured up the written word around 5,000 years ago, and that created a whole new profession: Writer.

I have always thought of myself as a storyteller first and a writer second, due to a lack of formal education in the latter, but, if I am a writer at all, my stories have been about my travels, so call me a travel writer.

Travel writing is big business these days, even though it took a while to stand shoulder to shoulder with its haughtier cousin...li-ter-a-ture...but, acknowledgment is confirmation. Today, travel writing holds its place among the very best literature, and many of its practitioners rank among the finest writers on Earth. But, this travel writer would argue that our kind has been enlightening and entertaining the world from the very early days.

As proof, I would offer Pausanias who left behind a most readable travelogue of his Greek homeland back in the second century. Granted, since then, almost eight centuries passed before we got the first Lonely Planet Guide, but, travel writing really gained some altitude in 1145 when Ibn Jubayr, hailing from what is now modern Spain, published his travel journals to great public acclaim. If only he had some slides to show with them. That account was most likely read by another Ibn, named Battuta, who spent the following 30 years roaming the then known world and sharing it with one and all in his epic work, Rihlah, the

Arabic word for "journey." It is still popular today. After Mister Battuta, our kind proliferated like rabbits.

From the double Battutas to Mark Twain, from Freya Stark to Tim Cahill, travel writers have been capturing our planet, its places and people, in words, and bringing all of it home to those who are unable, unwilling, or simply disinclined to venture forth on their own. Travel writers are artists who have chosen words as their medium rather than paint or clay, and whose work will stand the test of time just as the works of Michelangelo and Bernini.

To those among you who prefer an armchair to an airline seat, I say, "Bravo!" I have always hated crowds when I travel, and the fewer of us there are out there, the more of you there are to buy our books about where you have not been. And to those hardcore travelers among you who do journey into the world and still read other peoples' stories about where you have been, God bless you!

But whether you are a world cruiser or couch potato, please consider why travel is so important. It is easy to form a stereotype of someone from a thirty-second sound bite on the evening news, but difficult to hate that same person when you have shaken their hand and looked them in the eye. To quote the venerable Mr. Twain, "Travel is fatal to prejudice, bigotry, and narrow-mindedness, and many of our people need it sorely on these accounts."

For me, travel has always been a learning process in my continuing education. It has also been the great equalizer and antidote to a privileged Western lifestyle. While I would not want to trade places with someone who lives in a mud or grass hut, I have yet to meet a person who lived in one who would prefer my life to their own. Travel has taught me that wherever we come from, whatever our social status, our home is our home and no one way of living is any better than another; they are all simply different.

Travel has shown me that some of the most materially poor are among the happiest and most spiritually blessed of people, and many have made me think long and hard about my own life and how I live it, while a few of them have actually enlightened me enough to make personal changes. Travel has taught me to slow down and appreciate the world around me. It has gifted me with the ability to see a ballet in the jump of a fish, and hear an aria in the chirp of a cricket.

Travel has taught me not to judge people by the color of their skin or the way they dress, because that guy sleeping under the overpass may be a down on his luck astrophysicist, and the girl serving your chili fries might be a great poet.

There are countless cultures out there right now that will disappear with little of the world ever knowing they existed, and they are doing so at an alarming rate. The great anthropologist Wade Davis has suggested that the final speaker of a language passes from this earth every week, and when that happens, it takes an entire culture with it. That, to quote an old African saying is, "like a library burning." The death of each of these cultures leaves a hole in our collective consciousness, and while the current world order is in no immediate threat of collapse, each time one small part of it goes; it tears a page from the story of mankind.

I have spent two thirds of my life wandering the most remote places in order to meet my brothers and sisters, learn about their lives, and to share them with interested readers. If by "walking a mile in their shoes," I have stirred your imagination enough for you to want to go and see new places for yourself, then I have been successful.

So, I am a storyteller and these are my stories. Their real success is if you, the reader, enjoy them. They span almost four decades of my wandering, mostly in places few others wish to go. The more I have traveled the more I have developed a sense of obligation to share what I have experienced, especially from places few others have seen. Visiting remote cultures, mostly those with no written language, has given me a sense of purpose to provide such people with a voice, even though it is a tiny one, it is a voice to tell the world, "We exist!"

Now come with me and I will take you around the world.

Introduction

JAMES DORSEY IS A RARE COMBINATION: SWASHBUCKLING adventurer and spiritual seeker, whose immersion in the traditions, histories, and people of places near and far, ignite transformation over and over again.

Infused with humor, insight, and heart, each story contains a scene when time slows and James goes deep into the moment to truly transport readers. We swelter in the Danakil Desert, shiver on a ledge in a cave underneath Budapest, gaze at the stars above Kilimanjaro, and face a shrieking baboon in Tanzania.

But this book does much more than merely transport. In *Baboons for Lunch*, during the day we hang out with ancient tribesmen and wise elders, ascend a staircase {under unique fire}in Burma, meet a monk at Angkor Wat who survived the Khmer Rouge, are pursued through the Marrakech souk, and imbibe with a bootlegger in Laos and a Russian grandmother. And at night, the characters, images, and scenes that so often haunt Dorsey's dreams now visit ours as well and we become as James writes, "Captured by a vortex beyond comprehension."

—Erin Byrne,
author of *Wings: Gifts of Art, Life and Travel in France*
editor of *Vignettes and Postcards from Morocco*
editor of *Vignettes and Postcards from Paris*

PART ONE

Humorous
Travels

Techno monks

Monks and Monkey Poop on the Mountain

AT FIRST SIGHT, THE TEMPLE ON THE MOUNTAIN SEEMED A folk tale come to life.

On my journey through Burma, the gleaming temple on the rock that guards Mount Popa, had become my challenge, my grail, my pilgrimage, and there it towered above me like a finger of God pointing toward heaven.

Taung Kalat, the sacred monastery, is the jewel atop 777 stairs of a sheer tower of andesite basalt that rises 2,400 feet, the dramatic remains of a prehistoric eruption; a gleaming temple on the summit. From afar it brings to mind a giant termite mound. The summit monastery was attended to solely by the Buddhist hermit monk U Khandi for many years, and is still watched over by a palace guard of sacred monkeys. It is also the ethereal abode of the 37 most powerful of Burmese Nats, the spirits of local Buddhism. In a religion-dominated society, it is a major point of pilgrimage, and if any karma by association was available, Taung Kalat was the place to find it.

The village epicenter was a single, mud-lined street, whose stalls offered cheap plastic trinkets that clashed with the religious fervor of pilgrims on hands and knees. Many have crossed the country in this glacially slow fashion, arriving in torn rags but with flaming souls. Many will not stand fully upright until reaching the temple of Taung Kalat.

I removed my shoes and socks and bought an offering of burning sage for what I hoped would be a day of spiritual renewal, with a pinch of enlightenment thrown in. I entered the line of faithful and had just taken the first step when the stench hit me, and looking at the towering staircase above, realized I was about to climb through 2,000 feet of monkey poop.

It was everywhere; on the steps, the bannisters, the walls; impossible to go around. Apparently sacred monkeys don't give a damn about hygiene, and while it might sound a bit crude to use both ubiquitous and poop in the same sentence, it is appropriate here. Fortunately, I could also see a vast fleet of tiny women all robed in what might be hazmat suits scrubbing everywhere in what must be a nonstop job. Either way I had come in search of peace and knowledge and was not about to be defeated by mere monkey feces. As I ascended the stairs, I was totally unprepared for one of the scrubbing women to thrust out her hand and demand money; after all, I had paid an entry fee with the implied caveat that it included a poop removal surcharge. But, after each step, another blue rubber glove shot out at me all of which I declined until I felt and heard simultaneously the dull thud of a ball of monkey poop striking my posterior.

I wheeled around to confront the sisterhood of rubber-clad maidens that had attacked me for failure to pay up and that is when I saw the first monkey. He was big and mean and had a Donald Trump scowl. He was also holding a fistful of feces that he rolled around in his hands like a pitcher rubbing up a new ball, and just as he let fly in my direction, I noticed eight or nine hundred of his compatriots had surrounded me. It did not help that the idiot climbing behind me had opened a large bag of hard candy and was dumping it on the ground so he could take photos of the swarming monkeys. You could hear his scream across the valley as they stripped his camera, watch, and ring; like sharks with blood in the water. I tucked my camera under my shirt, put my head down, and began climbing as fast as I could go and thought I might be away from ground zero when the second ball of poop hit me.

Those monkeys were the most efficient crew of pirates I have yet encountered, and that includes the Gypsies of Rome. One had to marvel how they came at you in waves, one distracting you, while the others swarm and relieve you of any possession that is not part of your anatomy, and then trying to take some that are. They grabbed at my shirt buttons when I had nothing else to offer but I managed to keep my camera tucked away as those same nimble fingers continued to hurl feces with major league accuracy.

With aching knees and filthy feet I emerged from the endless stairs into a brilliant blue sky 2,400 feet above where I started. My feet looked like they were encased in cement but the view in all directions defied words. I began to circle the summit walkway only to notice a distinct lack of monkeys, and that is when I saw the first monks.

They came out of the sun, silhouettes, like bandits in an aerial dogfight. Once again I could say ubiquitous as it sounds better here than it did with poop, because they were everywhere. That is not unusual in a Buddhist country, but these monks were not acting very monkly. There was no meditation or contemplation going on. These were not your cloistered, chanting, alms begging monks; they were techno monks! Photo monks! Everywhere I looked there were monks taking photos with iPhones, iPads, and some even with actual cameras! They took pictures of each other that looked exactly the same! Those not taking photos were texting on their smartphones. Nor were they observing any vows of silence. In fact they were the noisiest people in the temple. It looked and sounded like a Silicon Valley toga party. For a country just emerging from four centuries behind the rest of the world, these guys were making up for lost time. I assumed they would not act this way at their own monastery, so they were visitors, monks on vacation as it were. Apparently I had discovered spring break for monks.

No sooner had I stepped out onto a balcony, than I was besieged by saffron-robed, shaved-headed teenagers with selfie sticks. Now at that time, the ruling military junta of Burma had just begun to open the national doors to people like me, and westerners were indeed an exotic rarity in remote places like Taung Kalat, but I quickly transcended rarity status to become an instant celebrity as dozens of monks and their families descended on me like a plague of wide angle locusts.

The monks, like the monkeys, came at me in waves, and so, for over an hour after I reached the summit, I posed for and smiled at various electronic devices, arms around tiny people wearing orange sheets and wondering how they tell each other apart; still unable to savor the beauty of the temple interior, and certainly not achieving any peace or tranquility. There was also a touch of degradation as I was at least a foot taller than anyone who stood next to me that day, making me feel like the extended middle finger of a fist.

Once inside, the interior of the temple was a curious blend of beautiful traditional statuary and painting, juxtaposed with gaudy Christmas tree lights and Las Vegas neon bling so often found in remote shrines. Haloes circled Buddha heads, changing colors in clockwise direction, and flashing strings of lights illuminated every doorframe and window. Elaborately clothed mannequins stand in for the ethereal Nats, their images, looking like conglomerate Halloween costumes, standing over piles of food and money. To one unfamiliar with Southeast Asia, such scenes can project a carnival-like atmosphere, but in fact, it is all done with purpose and deep reason. Sometimes the gaudiest is also the most fervent.

But even in this, the holiest of holies, there was no respite. Everyone wanted their photo with me and the nonstop flashes were blinding. I was feeling overwhelmed until the blonde walked in. She was tall and elegant as only a Scandinavian could be, and her sudden presence stopped the monks in their barefoot tracks. There was an audible group gasp as she tossed her mane-like tresses in the wind and stood there posed like a silhouette on a truckers' mud flap. Even her perfect sandaled feet were clean of any monkey poop. In the blink of an eye I was replaced by a Nordic goddess. She floated through the temple like a gazelle, smiling at one and all as dozens of tiny shaved heads swiveled at her passing. She was working the room as though it was a Vegas lounge and not a Buddhist temple. Now, I am sure any good Buddhist would tell you that such behavior is disrespectful at best, but at that moment, I think the monks were just fine with it.

Suddenly, as if a silent whistle had been sounded, a massed throng of monks engulfed the young woman, solidly pinning her against a large smiling Buddha, which made me wonder if he had been smiling prior to that. Certainly by now, the sacred Nats must be smiling too.

A line was quickly formed and selfies were flying fast and furious. I took advantage of the diversion to stage my retreat. In my final look back, I saw that Pre-Raphaelite face smiling above a sea of bald heads, looking like a lawn statue surrounded by garden gnomes, an image that will linger a while.

But, I still had to get down, and I was ready for the monkeys during my descent. I had picked up a discarded pair of rubber gloves on the way; hygiene be damned. I then scooped up as much dung as I could hold and began to mold the perfect poop ball because I would not go quietly into the night. But, while I was molding the poop in my hands, it occurred to me that I had come to this place in search of peace and perhaps a little enlightenment, and there I was preparing to do hand-to-hand combat with a monkey. I needed to rethink the moment.

Trump was there with his drooping leer when I arrived, projectile in hand, ready for launch. I looked him in the eye and that is something I have always been told never to do with a monkey. I dropped my dung ball and slowly raised my empty hands in surrender. He lowered his dung ball, not out of deference to me, but because he was suddenly distracted by an empty yogurt container blowing by in the wind. To him, even that was more interesting than I was at the moment, so suddenly no one wanted to take my photo and no monkey wanted to blast me with his poop. I had achieved insignificance, and isn't that a major goal of Buddhism? Until that moment, I had always thought my great moment of enlightenment would be a bit more epic, but, you take what you can get.

I had gone to Taung Kalat in search of the spiritual and it was certainly there, just buried under several tons of dung. Most of the locals who live near the mountain spend their lives in service to Buddha as either a monk or nun, and their culture was already ancient when mine was being born. Many of them have climbed the stairs for years, sometimes on hands and knees, and all have offered prayers and entreaties to the 37 sacred Nats housed on the summit. My presence happened to be a rare and different distraction, but it was never meant to disrupt.

While the monkeys seemed comical to me, to the local population, they are sacred. They are their own selves on a lower evolutionary plane and believe that climbing the stairs with them adds to their karma to come back as a person in another life. When the monkeys act out, it is the Nats using them to admonish the people for their various transgressions. There are holy men within the temple who smear themselves with the dung both as a protection and a reminder that they are but equals with their simian cousins. Such is Buddhism.

Enlightenment does not come in a day or a month, or even a lifetime for most of us, and it is certainly not attainable simply by visiting places or people. I seek these places not expecting to find answers, but because everyone there seems to have a slightly better handle on that aspect of life than I do, and I'm always hoping for a little bit of that to come my way. If it comes coated with monkey dung, that is just fine with me.

The perfect shot

Me and Tea in Burma

WHENEVER I LOOK UP, THE TRAIL MERCIFULLY FADES INTO the clouds above, obscuring all distance.

The word "trail" is used loosely here, as the term, in my mind at least, at least should refer to a walkable surface associated with hiking. This churned quagmire of mud and loose rocks does not even vaguely meet that definition. The jungle of northern Burma is hostile enough, but I am pushing a titanium hip and deteriorating knee to their limits here. For two hours we have been steadily climbing through a cotton candy haze that has me asking myself, "Why?"

I stop to suck air, bent in half, and Pin's smiling face pushes next to mine as he whispers, "Close now," a term I have come to associate with local guides that means "We are hell and gone from where we should be."

Pin is a dead ringer for a young Jackie Chan, but has never seen a movie, so he does not understand when I mime a scene from *Rush Hour*. He just looks at me and rolls his eyes, but his irresistible smile is a fixture. "Not much further," he says, and his words make me laugh. I tell myself the hill tribe I have come to see will be worth the effort.

Pin distracts my aching knees along the way by pointing out minute details of flora and fauna and touches my soul when he bends to cup a large moth, stuck in the mud, into his hands. He gently carries it to the side of the trail and sets it on a rock to dry in the sun; for him, an act natural as breathing, but revealing to me the essence of this Buddhist country.

Four hours into our "two-hour hike" we have breached the clouds and the lush summits of ancient peaks surround us in all directions. It feels as though I am on the roof of the world. I get a first glimpse of the village on the neighboring mountainside across the valley; a collection of stilted shacks clinging to an impossibly vertical slope seemingly held in place only by the surrounding jungle. It is a speck of civilized progress gouged into a prehistoric landscape and it appears to still be several miles away. In my exhaustion, I do not even ask its' name. "Almost there," Pin whispers through his smile.

Far below us green patches of rice paddies peak through gaps in the clouds and I see tiny brown specks of water buffalo grazing. If I weren't so tired it would be quite beautiful. Suddenly a crimson robed monk comes bouncing down the trail with the spring of youth in his step. He is wearing straw sandals and carrying a rice bowl. He smiles broadly as he passes us and Pin joins his hands in the prayer position, touching them to his forehead to show respect. The monk can be no more than 12 or 13 years old, but in Burma, the red robes are revered. The descending boy is quickly swallowed by the clouds as if he were a dream.

An hour later barking dogs announce our arrival as I stumble into the village. I see curious shadows dart away from windows as we walk past the mud and brick houses.

There is a feeling of great age upon this place and the smell of cow dung fires and roasting corn floats on the air. I slosh through runoff from the previous evening rain and my splashing sends dozens of grasshoppers jumping a foot ahead, only to do so over and over again at my next step, reminding me of the endless karma of reincarnation. My mind seems to be searching for Buddhist metaphors so I do not concentrate on the pain.

We reach a shack that leans up hill to keep from tumbling down the mountainside and Pin has declared it a "tea house." The dirt in front of the entrance is stained a deep crimson from spit beetle juice. I bend over to clear the low ceiling as I step up and over the transom that keeps out snakes. Inside, the room is dark, holding a single long table and several benches. I drop my camera bag on the floor and slide onto a bench, anticipating food. The only light is through wall cracks and the door-less entranceway. The room carries hints of curry, and the stench of previous trekkers. Most of all, it smells of tea.

I should say here and now that I hate tea! That includes the hundreds of exotic brands my friends have plied me with over the years intending to make me like it. They are convinced there is yet that elusive brand out there with my taste buds written on it. I think not. So, I am not happy to find myself in a tea house after climbing a mountain for five hours. I had visions of seared goat and maybe some rice. At least a cold beer!! I can't smell any meat cooking but I do smell tea. My brief wallow in self-pity ends when the Amah walks through a pulled curtain like a Smithsonian photograph come to life. Amah is a term that approximates the word "grandmother" in several languages and one I have come to apply often to elderly ladies I have just met.

She is a vision, an elder of the Palang people, a Burmese hill tribe that lives the old way on the sides of mountains not yet invaded by technology. Her native garb is colorful as a flower garden and her skin like old saddle leather. Beetle nut stains her toothy smile and she immediately enchants my camera. She is the essence of the people I have come to see. The Palang are known for their textiles and this lady is a walking museum piece. She is enough to make me forget about food until I notice she is carrying a tray of tea.

She pours me a cup and I hope she will not notice that I ignore it. My image of a dignified tribal elder is damaged when she begins chittering in a high-pitched staccato voice. Shrill as a chipmunk she begins frantically hauling out large bags of clothing that she dumps on the table for me to buy. I am a giant here and wealthy beyond local comprehension, so this is not unusual. One or two American dollars will feed a family for days. I try to photograph her as she flits about like a bumblebee collecting pollen but she moves too quickly. She is holding clothing up to my western girth and commenting in her native Riang about my size, realizing nothing she has will fit this huge visitor while loudly bemoaning her loss of potential sales. I physically stop her in the doorway whose filtered light hides half her face in shadow, and I take my first decent portrait before she darts away.

Myanmar has only been open to travelers for about four years and cameras are still an unknown quantity in many rural villages. She seems to have no concept of what I am doing and begins to wind a colorful swath of textile around my head while she chatters on. Her energy is manic, and so, to calm her down I ask Pin to tell her I will buy this head wrap if she will just stop long enough for me to photograph her. He says "Yes" but then he has said yes so many times I am not sure how far his English extends beyond that single word. He continues to smile but says nothing to the lady.

While the Amah dumps another bag of clothing on the table searching for super extra-large, I open a door to investigate a delicious aroma coming from the next room, a glorious smell that tickles my nose and overrides the stench of tea. There I see my ultimate photo waiting to be taken.

A single shaft of afternoon sunlight drifts lazily through the open window, mingling with the smoke from a wood fire. It angles downward to showcase a water kettle on the burning embers and suspended above it are two large wicker flats, one on top of the other, each holding an assortment of corn, squash, nuts, and other delicacies slowly roasting over the open fire. The smoke and light shaft combine to dull all edges, giving the room an impressionistic quality, as if viewing the scene through a silk veil. The background is dark and shadowy while the foreground is that mystical, medieval light that gifts unforgettable photos. It is a Renaissance painting waiting for its Madonna. All I have to do to make it happen is endure some tea and buy some old clothes.

I smack my head on an overhead beam in my eagerness to drag the Amah into the room and am grateful it is wrapped with her textiles even though I must look ridiculous. I realize that to her, I appear gigantic, with one glass eye in the middle of my face, my head wrapped in a towel, bent almost in half to walk, and I am frantically pointing at the fire, trying to move her into the fragile light before it is gone. She slowly sidesteps into the filtered aura with a confused look, but I know she has been photographed before when she assumes that ramrod straight posture many indigenous people think photographers want but actually hate. I am waiving my arms, trying to tell her how I want her posed in the light shaft. I ask Pin to tell her to just kneel and tend the fire naturally and he smiles and says "Yes." I am getting no help whatsoever from Jackie Chan.

Finally the Amah gets it and squats down. She picks up a long bamboo tube and begins to blow on the embers. This is it! This is what I came for! It is a once in a lifetime shot that the Creator occasionally gives to those of us who climb impossible mountains for hours only to end up in tea houses with no food.

I am kneeling down low, about to click the shutter when I am elbowed from the side and tumble into a pile of rice bags. I look up and see several cameras flashing at my Amah! What the hell is going on?

Several trekkers have arrived minutes after me, looking for a bathroom, when they stumble onto my masterpiece in progress and butt right in. They are noisy Europeans, rudely shooting without asking permission. The old Amah looks like a deer in the headlights as half a dozen flashes obliterate the moody light of the room. In their rush to capture the image, they are destroying it.

I hold my temper and wait them out. Finding no bathroom, they quickly lose interest and retreat to the next room to swig tea as noisily as they arrived. The Amah and I stare at each other for a second and we are both thinking, "What just happened here?"

My Amah starts to follow them realizing she now has smaller customers that her clothes will fit, but I grab her hand and motion her toward the fire. We are alone now and I shut the door. The photo is waiting for us to take it. She has finally picked up on what I am after, sensing the possibility of the moment. She turns off the saleswoman and segues into my ballet partner. She kneels with the grace of a mountain dove and tenderly stokes the flame like a mother caressing a child. Her actions are ethereal as she leans in to blow on the fire; the Madonna has entered the painting. She moves almost unperceptively as I shoot, over and over, each image an icon. We are both in the moment now, totally in sync, and for a few precious seconds, photographer and model merge to create an intimate work of art.

I shoot dozens of takes and when I stand up to give my aching knees a break I bang my head on a sagging beam and she laughs. The moment is gone but the magic lingers. I help her to her feet and we return to the next room to find the trekkers trying on various bits of her clothing. The Amah is happy with this windfall of sales and resumes her manic chattering as she collects her money. She turns to look at me and I sense she knows something special has just taken place. I sip tea and we smile at each other. I still hate the tea. Jackie Chan is smiling and nodding his head, "Yes."

I place money on the table and offer a slight bow to the Amah who returns it with a broad smile. I step outside into a brilliant sun and think that the trail down the mountain will be much shorter now.

Jackie Chan looks at me and I nod to him and say, "Yes."

The Communist governor giving a toast

Commies, Crickets, and Kitties in China

PIERRE WAS AN OLD CHINA HAND AND NO ONE KNEW THE country better. The fact that he had been arrested numerous times for wandering into restricted regions gave me no pause when he invited me on the latest adventure. "What can go wrong?" he said and I stupidly agreed.

On this journey we delivered much needed medical supplies to a remote hospital in the far northwest; Xinjiang province, land of the Uyghur people on the northern Silk Road. That bought us permission to explore areas not usually open to tourists, permission being something Pierre usually did not bother with anyway. Afterward, Chinese etiquette required our hosts, all elevated cadre of the local Communist party, to thank us properly in the form of a sumptuous banquet and we humbly accepted.

An official car picked us up at our hotel. We thought we were going to a local restaurant so I had my usual three cameras with me, but within minutes we were cruising through rolling countryside, leaving the city of Urumqi behind. An hour later we arrived at what was obviously a military base. There must be some mistake, I thought, as uniformed guards snapped to attention and saluted while we motored through the towering gates without slowing down.

One of the cardinal rules of traveling in China, or any police state, is to avoid military bases, especially when carrying cameras, but there I was, a Western capitalist and writer, inside a Communist military installation with my bag full of what could potentially be perceived as spy tools. This was supposed to be a simple thank you dinner so how in hell could this be happening? Only later would I learn that many of the finest restaurants in northwestern China are reserved for Communist officials: this one, in the middle of nowhere, just happened to be on an air force base.

A lone fighter jet screeched overhead like a banshee as we stepped out of the car into a swarming mass of feral cats. We dared not move until an overweight soldier in tight fitting uniform ushered them out of our way with his boot before coming to attention and saluting us with his rifle. A line of soldiers, descending in height from tallest to shortest stood wilting in the afternoon heat, looking like a selection of Russian nesting dolls. They turned as one, formed a phalanx around us, and began marching us to what I assumed would be my place of interrogation if not my execution. Instead, we were ushered to meet the military governor of Xinjiang province who was surprisingly attired in casual, western style, civilian clothing. He seemed out of place in his Tommy Bahama shirt, and he was wearing the obligatory mirrored aviator shades so favored by self-important political appointees in developing countries.

"Welcome," he said, sticking out a beefy hand to shake. "You are not writers or spies are you?" And with that he and his entourage of yes men began to chuckle and I felt weak. I figured he had taken a peek at my website before our arrival and knew that I was a writer. Nothing could save me now.

My knuckles whitened around my camera bag in a death grip, hoping to absorb it, praying I might be rescued by a stroke or heart attack, when several of the officials' wives appeared with cameras and began taking selfies with us. Realizing my execution was no longer imminent, I allowed myself to relax. Mrs. Communist Governor, a pretty, stylish lady with a high-pitched voice, spoke in a nasal twang that would be the Chinese equivalent of a southern drawl. She also reeked of strong rice wine. She attached herself to my arm like a paid escort and I realized she needed something to hold onto before she fell off her towering heels.

Inside the yurt, there was one large, circular table, covered in white with formal place settings, both with knives, forks, and chopsticks at each seat. The governor sat on an elevated chair as we took our places around him like vassals of the king. Near the entrance, uniformed men tended plastic buckets of strange creatures that I assumed were about to become our meal. I could identify eels and scorpions and did not really want to know the species of some others. The overweight soldier whose tunic buttons threatened to explode off his uniform walked around offering a tray of fried unidentifiable critters, balled up in the fetal position that I could not bring myself to pop into my mouth. In the center of the table sat a massive bowl of sunflower seeds, obviously a local favorite, as everyone shoveled them in like popcorn while loudly spitting out the husks onto the carpet-covered floor where cats pounced on them to lick the salt. Multiple bottles of local rice wine were the final table accessories.

Almost falling into her chair next to me, the governor's wife, Li Mai, spoke excellent although slightly slurred English. She had obviously had quite a few before our arrival. She also had a diplomat's polish and was adept at small talk while putting her guest at ease. She asked all the right questions about family and home, turning away briefly every now and then to speak to her other dining partner, but always returning her attention to me, and all the while spitting long streams of sunflower husks ten feet across the floor. Her eloquence suggested a fine education, but from the way she formed her questions, I guessed her knowledge of most things came from the official party line and not from worldly experience. Twice she leaned in close, almost nose to nose, and held my gaze until it became uncomfortable. At first I could not tell if it was just boozy flirting, as that was the last thing I needed, but I got the sense that she needed to talk with someone other than her usual entourage. Her social position and isolated location must have made for a lonely life.

She narrated our dinner for me, announcing that on the platter before us were baked baby sparrows, plucked and curled into little round balls, and lathered with what appeared to be a sauce so hot I could see heat waves coming off it. Now I have never been a particularly adventurous eater, especially when so far off the beaten path, but to not eat would have been a terrible insult to my hosts.

The next dish didn't offer a reprieve. Li Mai informed me that it was rabbit embryo, or at least that is what it sounded like as she downed another rice wine, though I never would have guessed it from the writhing mass on the platter: formless blobs with eyes, it resembled a predigested meal. Pierre was no help as he will eat whatever is put in front of him and had his back to me, deep in conversation with the governor.

I gained some face by my adeptness with chopsticks but most of the diners were eating with their fingers, snatching delicacies straight of the platters. I watched them digging in, holding the birds by beak and feet while turning them like miniature corncobs and crunching tiny bones to suck out the marrow. All around me, little beaks protruded from peoples' mouths as they sucked brains out of the backs of tiny skulls.

I kept the conversation going with Li Mai, trying to distract her so she would not notice that I had ceased eating and was merely moving food about on my plate. Every now and then, when she would look the other way, I would slip a bite of whatever into my lap napkin to reduce the volume on my plate. It also helped that round after round of rice wine toasts were being offered and the liquor was adding to the volume of table conversation. When it came my turn to offer a toast I mumbled something about international friendship, that when translated, brought a round of cheers and everyone threw back another round. That is when I felt a sharp pain in my leg.

I reached under the table thinking perhaps a spider had bitten me when my hand felt the furry back of a tiny kitten, one of the many feral cats that were not supposed to be allowed inside the dining yurt. No one had seen it slip in and now it was digging its claws into my leg, asking for food. As far as I was concerned, it was sent as my guardian angel. Moving slowly, I slid my napkin down to the hungry animal. The little scavenger was ravenous and I could clearly hear it chomping away on my discarded food, but the general sounds of the table drowned it out.

I continued to covertly pass it tiny wings, feet, and various other body parts. The kitten did its best to vacuum up food as quickly as I could feed it, and our hosts, sucking up the wine as though it were going extinct, appeared none the wiser about my secret helper. I had been saved.

We got a rhythm going, the cat and I, working as a team. In a few seconds we were an assembly line, as efficient as a McDonalds drive-through, working at full tilt as I picked up body parts with my chopsticks and conveniently dropped them into my lap napkin on the way to my mouth, grateful for the alcohol that was making the dining crowd oblivious to everything but their immediate meal.

That is when the cat belched. It was a very loud belch, loud enough for most of the table to hear it over the general cacophony, especially Li Mai who laughed and slipped a drunken arm over my shoulder. I would not have thought such an epic sound could issue from such a tiny animal, but just then, it sounded to me like trumpets before the walls of Jericho. I slumped in my chair asking God to swallow me into the earth. Then the Governor got up slowly on very unstable legs and I figured he was about to call for his troops to haul me away when he raised his glass in my direction, and offered a formal toast.

Everyone came to their feet while Li Mai motioned for me to remain seated. The governor thought that I was the belcher, and that I was paying compliments to one and all, and he said how considerate it was for a foreigner to know so much about their ways. With that, everyone raised their glass to me as I felt my lily white Western face turning bright red. The kitten had not only saved me from dinner, but had given me great face by complimenting the meal. Minor as that incident was on the world stage, I doubt that any animal has ever done more for Sino-American relations with a simple bodily function.

As the evening wound down, I managed to fortify myself with handfuls of sunflower seeds as I had not eaten anything else all day. Pierre and I paid our respects, and as we climbed into the car for the ride back to the city, I was surprised when Li Mai got in beside me holding a glass of wine for the road, saying she was joining us as she had business to attend to the following day in town.

I was lost in thought for several minutes, realizing I had narrowly missed causing an international incident, but had met high-ranking Communist officials and photographed them inside a military installation. Instead of being executed, I might have a good story to tell. All in all, it was quite a coup and I was feeling rather full of myself.

That is when Li Mai rolled up the security window so the driver could not hear us and said to me, "I could not eat much of that stuff either. Why don't we stop and get a burger on the way?"

Then she turned and purred to Pierre, "So, are you married?"

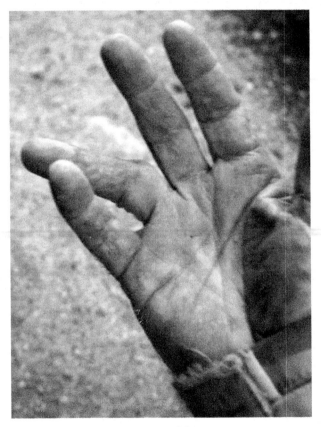

My wayward finger

Burrowing
Beneath
Budapest

TRAVEL WRITING CAN BE A DANGEROUS PROFESSION, ESPE-
cially when you are staying in a luxury hotel.

It was my final two days at the venerable Gellart in
Budapest, a grand and aging old world hangout of the rich
and famous whose rooms are each named for the illustri-
ous personages that have occupied them.

I wanted photos of the hotel's subterranean mineral
baths for a magazine article and was up at the crack of
dawn to take them before anyone would be bathing, so
imagine my surprise when I walked in with my camera to
find it occupied by two dozen naked and very hairy men.
No one told me that the wee hours were when the city's
municipal workers occupied the baths for free.

We all froze in place; they, staring at my camera; and
me, staring at shortcomings I had no desire to see so early
in the morning, if ever. In that finite moment, when an
illogical image from a crisis fixes itself in your mind, it
struck me that all of the gentlemen before me had very

large mustaches. Without lingering on that thought, I beat a hasty retreat as various threats of violence were being hurled my way.

Not yet realizing the severity of my faux pas, I made it as far as the concierge desk before it dawned on me that I could not show my face again anywhere in the hotel without fingers pointing at the resident pervert. I was saved by a brochure on the concierge's desk.

It seems that Budapest sits atop a massive system of caves, carved over the eons by swift-flowing thermal springs, the very same springs that feed the baths that I had just fled. The brochure advertised three different sets of caves that were open to the public for tours. With my wife giggling about my early morning encounter, she informed me that she could occupy the baths with impunity, and intended to spend the day doing so. I hopped on a bus to spend my final hours in a cave where I would still get a travel story and hopefully not be accused of any sex crimes. An hour later, I was deposited at a comfortable-looking station in the green rolling hills that surround Budapest.

I entered what appeared to be a massive locker room to find myself in the middle of eight young and totally buff bodies, both men and women, all of them no more than half my age in various stages of undress. I was instantly grateful that I was not holding my camera, but wondering how and why it was that I kept walking in on naked people.

A moment later, I found out that of the three different cave systems, two of them were guided walking tours that required about an hour of leisure strolling among the stalactites and stalagmites, while the third one, the one I was about to enter, was down in the dirt, crawling through cracks and crevices with a miner's hardhat and lamp into alcoves where only a rodent should tread.

While my fellow explorers snickered at this aging addition to their group they also began to help me suit up in overalls, boots, gloves, hard hat with lamp, and jumar ascenders...curious hand-held devices that resemble brass knuckles but allow you to lock onto a rope easily while moving up or down.

Now I had never done any spelunking as it is officially called, but assumed that with so many young athletes around me I would be in good company, and within minutes we were walking through the forest in anticipation. We stopped at an ancient and rusting steel door in the side of a rock wall that our leader opened with an equally ancient looking skeleton key the size of a spatula. The door creaked and moaned as it slowly revealed total darkness inside and we all turned on our headlamps as we entered. Our leader was called Rat and I am not sure if that was his true name or just a moniker based on his resemblance to the rodents that I was about to share space with. Rat was old school. His miner's hat held a candle in front of a mirror for light and he had callouses on his knuckles the size of golf balls. He was also stick thin with hands like baseball gloves, built for caving, while I am rather large and built more for lounging by the pool.

Immediately inside the door, the outer world disappeared and we had entered a separate reality...grim, cold, and dark. I was standing on a narrow ledge next to Rat, and one step forward was a drop into black nothingness. The Rat, who only spoke Hungarian, attached his jumars to a long rope and slid into the darkness like he was on a firehouse pole, leading by example. We all followed, one by one. It was easier than I had expected with the jumars locking in place when I applied pressure to them and loosening to let me slide down when I released pressure. At the bottom, a good 30 feet below the entrance, we stood pressed together while I watched Rat slither into a hole no larger than a small beach ball, and I wondered what had I gotten myself into.

I watched his feet kicking and twisting like a hooked trout as he fought his way through an impossibly small tunnel. Just as the first wave of panic overtook me, I laid out flat like Superman in flight, arms straight out, and slid downward as though I were on a waterslide and not in a subterranean hole. With the eight of us now in the bowels of the cave, our headlamps produced eerie shadows that danced around us like evil spirits wishing to drag us to hell. Our voices were magnified in the narrow caverns and echoed down passageways that had never known the tread of a human. For the next hour we continued our descent as I fought the urge to flee; slipping, sliding, and squeezing through ever smaller openings that threatened each time to trap me in place forever.

I was holding onto the top edge of a large boulder and sliding my hands along as though hanging from a ledge while trying to position my feet for a good hold when I heard a loud pop and lost my grip, falling in a heap that raised a choking dust cloud of what was probably bat guano. When I looked down my right ring finger was pointing in a different direction than the rest of my body. Now I have never had a broken bone in my life, and seeing my digit poised at such an odd angle, my first thought was that I had a compound fracture, an added bonus to having a panic attack while trapped deep underground with strange people I could not communicate with.

The Rat was quickly at my side viewing my deformed hand with amused detachment, when without warning he grabbed the finger and gave it a hard jerk straight out. I swallowed a scream of pain and pulled my hand away, but the Rats' maneuver accomplished nothing as my finger still pointed north while the rest of me was going south. Apparently he had seen too many medical shows on television and when he realized his impromptu treatment had failed he shrugged his shoulders as if to say, "What can you do?" Up to that point I barely felt the finger thanks to rushing adrenalin, but after Rat almost pulled it off, it hurt like hell.

Next I was blinded by a flash, as one by one my fellow spelunkers began kneeling next to my hand and taking selfies as though it were something totally cool. At least they were not naked photos. The finger was now throbbing terribly and if it was not broken before, I was sure it was after Rat's impromptu treatment. Rat gave me a thumbs up and pointed the rest of the group toward a yawning hole in the wall. It was then that I knew he was not giving me a sign of encouragement, but telling me I was on my own as he led the other cavers away to continue their descent. Apparently the needs of the many surpass that of the one and I was being abandoned to my fate. I suppose that was one of those pivotal moments when your life is supposed to flash before your eyes, but all I could think of was that maybe I was bleeding to death internally deep inside a cave while my wife sat at the hotel bar nursing a Hennessey and nodding her head politely at the bartenders' story about a pervert who tried to photograph naked men in the baths that morning.

There was only one way out so I was not worried about getting lost, but, climbing up rocks that I had previously slid down was no easy task with only one good hand. I kept banging my head and knocking my helmet off, cut my hands repeatedly on sharp edges, and jammed my mangled finger countless times. Slowly but surely I made my way back to the rope by the entrance. The jumar ascenders allowed me to negotiate the rope without much trouble and when I pushed the creaking steel door open, the blast of sunlight and fresh air almost knocked me over. A check of my watch revealed that it had taken me just over four hours to ascend from the cave but I felt a wave of accomplishment at having done so alone. By this time I was pretty sure that my finger was merely dislocated and not fractured as there was no discoloration that would indicate internal bleeding.

walked back to the locker/assembly room on the forest path. I flung open the door and as I did so everyone inside froze in place with looks of horror on their faces. Then I saw myself in a wall mirror, my face a mass of tiny cuts and bruises, hair matted with sweat, dirt, and grime, my overalls smeared with grit and torn in several places. I was a demon from the depths and looked far worse than I felt, but my extreme appearance and solo arrival must have announced that a catastrophe had befallen our intrepid group of spelunkers.

I raised my hand to explain my early return from the cave and a collective gasp of shock filled the room as I watched my errant finger waving about of its own volition, making its' own separate point from what I wanted to say. Four attendants rushed to my side, forcing me to lie down, and began stripping off my gear, apparently thinking me to be terribly injured.

Everyone was speaking at once, giving orders, asking me questions and yelling, but I understood nothing, and when I tried to say anything, a burly fellow put his finger to my lips to quiet me. Another girl was on the telephone yelling loudly while two men began to suit up and grab ropes in what I then realized was the start of a search-and-rescue operation for the rest of the cavers that were now believed to be in serious peril if still alive at all. I heard myself yelling that everyone was just fine but no one was listening or understood me in the general panic of Hungarian spoken triage.

One young man had been winding my mangled hand with a gauze bandage during all of this and when he stopped it looked as though my arm ended in a large white bowling ball. I made one final protest that I was all right just as I was being picked up and carried outside to a waiting taxi and thrust into the back seat. People yelled instructions at the driver as we pulled away.

The driver kept checking on me in the rear view mirror as we picked up speed and I tried to motion for him to slow down, but all he saw was the large white orb on the end of my arm and drove even faster, convinced now that this was a race of life or death. I unwound the ungainly bandages and when the driver saw my finger he let out a cry and hunched over the wheel, driving now with renewed determination. He was taking hair turns at dangerous speeds and the tires were screaming in protest as we entered the afternoon rush of Budapest. We zipped in and out of traffic with the abandon of those about to die, changing lanes in the blink of an eye, horn continuously honking, and the driver hanging halfway out the window to wave people out of our way. In the rearview mirror I could see the whites of his panicked eyes and prayed the police would stop, us but none appeared.

I watched the city of Budapest zip by in a blur until we hit a curb and bounced into the parking lot of an emergency hospital in a display of skidding tires. I jumped out quickly, grateful to have survived the ride and before I could search for money he waved me off toward the emergency entrance. Inside, I walked down several vacant corridors before finding a living person and if I had been truly injured I would have bled out before making human contact at this "emergency" hospital. Finally, in what appeared to be a lounge, I found two women in scrubs that I thought might be doctors. I simply held up my hand and one of them led me into a small examining room while still munching her sandwich, and then disappeared.

Within minutes four people with surgical masks and wearing stethoscopes entered the room. Each took turns examining my finger while chatting amongst themselves. They retreated as a group into an office next door where I heard the conversation escalate loudly. After several minutes a lady appeared and I heard English spoken for the first time that day. "You are foreigner. We cannot treat you unless you pay first," she said.

"Fine," I replied, and pulled out my wallet with a credit card.

No credit, cash!" she said.

"How much is it?' I asked.

"Nine dollars U.S.," she replied.

"Let's hear it for socialized medicine," I said. I dug through my pockets and found a crumpled ten spot. Keep the change" I laughed as I handed her the money but she did not understand.

With that she grabbed my hand and pulled my finger straight out with a quick jerk. I heard a loud pop, felt a brief flash of pain, and was whole once again. She splinted the finger and wrapped it in gauze that made it about ten inches long and now it looked like an albino banana.

The taxi driver had waited for me, relieved to see I was still alive, and took me back to the hotel, where I retreated into my room to relate the whole story to my wife who had assumed I had spent my day strolling underground among tourists. That evening we had a farewell dinner in the hotel dining room in low candlelight where I was sure no one from the baths would recognize me. The food was wonderful but my extended finger kept poking the mashed potatoes.

We decided to take our dessert in our room when my wife pointed out that a man with a large mustache had been staring at me intensely from across the dining room.

Temple viper and scorpion whiskey

Mekong
Moonshine

I WAS FALLING OFF THE MAP IN CENTRAL LAOS, GOING UPRIVER
on the down-flowing Mekong, through country that
made me feel like Joseph Conrad heading into his heart
of darkness.

As one who favors out-of-the-way attractions, my destination was a moonshiner I had heard of who worked
deep in the jungles north of Luang Prabang, and after several beers I shook hands with a river man who was willing
to buck the currents of the Mekong to take me there.

For two hours there was nothing but searing heat and
jungle—lush towering jungle of teak and bamboo—from
the waterline straight up two hundred feet. Trembling
tree branches betrayed invisible monkeys and occasionally
launched an egret skyward. Once a line of water buffalo
spooked at our approach while drinking, but mostly there
was just impenetrable green. Near shore several dragon-
flies came to give us a look, floating on the breeze that
skated over the river where ladies in wide brimmed hats
stood on boulders and dipped umbrella nets over and over
to scoop up countless minnows while puffing on massive cigars. My attention was fixed on those boulders that

broke the waterline every few yards causing numerous jet-
ties that can instantly become whirlpools. It was extreme
country and yet I knew countless people lived in there,
invisible to most of the world. I was looking for one.

My river man put me ashore in the middle of nowhere,
on a rotting bamboo walkway on stilts that disappeared
into a decaying old village, saying he would return for me
that evening. That is as good as a traveler can get for an
agreed-upon time in the jungle. I walked as though treading on butterflies, expecting at any moment for the thing
to collapse under my weight and deposit me in the feces-
colored Mekong. At the top of the ramp was everything I
had come to see.

It was a full scale moonshine operation from a rice pro-
cessor to a homemade still and all stops in between, run by
a gentleman who called himself Kamdee, or maybe it was
Bambee, as it was hard to tell from his drunken slur. He
had obviously been testing his brew for quality control.
He bid me sit down and immediately handed me a shot
glass the size of a thimble of his homemade nectar; a glass
that I doubt had ever met soap. Now, had I walked in on
such an operation in the American Ozarks, or Appalachia,
I might have been met by a shotgun, but being the one
and only customer of the moment, in the middle of a
beastly wild jungle, I was more than welcome.

His clear nectar slid down my throat like lava to the sea
and I am sure my esophagus is scarred forever, but there
was an impeccably great aftertaste. It was the right mixture
of sour and sweet with enough fire to fuel a jet engine. As
moonshine goes, his was superior. I began to sweat and
took in my surroundings to buy time for my voice to start
working.

Under a shed that leaned dangerously downhill there
were numerous terra cotta pots of all sizes filled with fer-
menting rice, an old 50-gallon oil drum standing on end

over a wood fire acted as the still, with various scrap parts of garden hoses connecting everything. Several makeshift shelves held aging glass bottles filled with yellow liquid with what I assumed was formaldehyde and a ghoulish array of deceased snakes and rodents. Against another wall were turtle shells and animal skulls, horns, hooves and teeth. "Museum," was Mr. Kamdee's one word explanation. Mr. Kamdee handed me a second shot of his lethal work and began a running discourse in Lao that I assume was an explanation of his process. For those of us who are alcohol-distilling challenged, he had hung a crude drawing nearby that explained the process.

The finished whiskey flowed slowly out of the oil drum, down a used curtain rod, into a filthy rag that acted as a filter on its way into a jar, a most simple operation. The entire place was constructed of the detritus that most people would call junk, but in the jungle becomes most useful. In a nearby tree a young parrot eyed me with curiosity while a monkey of unidentifiable species offered its hind end to me in greeting. I thought it was going to urinate on me but Mr. Kamdee informed me that it was how Mr. Tojo asks for a drink, and with that he poured several small drops of whiskey into the monkey's thimble-sized bowl.

He lapped it up like a true boozer and pulled back his lips to reveal enormous teeth. I could not tell if he was smiling or gritting his teeth until the burn subsided. I went there fully prepared to drink with the man in order to get his story, but was not prepared for a monkey to make it a threesome. Monkeys are unpredictable at best, let alone drunken ones in the jungle. And what if the monkey could outdrink me? I would never live that down. As I pondered this potential challenge to my ego, Mr. Kamdee brought out the snake box.

Now, visitors to Southeast Asia are no stranger to what is locally called, "Cobra Whiskey." It is as ubiquitous as

phony antique opium pipes and bootlegged CDs of Sha-
kira. It is literally a bottle of whiskey with a cobra, scorpion, or temple viper, artfully stuffed inside and decorated
with tree sprigs to soften the look of a venomous predator
staring at you. It seems to be sold in every other store
throughout Southeast Asia and finding out how it was
made was my reason for being there. Locals will tell you it
is natural Viagra, the stuff of all-night erections and baby
booms. These are the same people that sell shark fins and
rhino horns to China as aphrodisiacs. They swear by it to
unwary tourists who have made it a best-selling item at
several airports. There were dozens of such bottles on display around the camp.

Mr. Kamdee opened the top of a large old Tupperware
box that was filled with various dead snakes, scorpions,
and several other critters I could not identify. It is best here
not to describe the stench of such a container in the heat
of the jungle. At the opening, Mr. Tojo, still smiling ear to
ear, retreated to a corner where he offered me his rear end
once again. I moved up and asked for another shot.

What I was getting from the fractured English of Mr.
Kamdee, was that he pays local kids a few cents each to
bring him venomous creepy crawlies to help flavor his
produce. With that he motioned for me to sit, gave me yet
another shooter of whiskey, and began to show me how
he placed deceased vipers into people's drinks. The snake
goes in tail first, slowly so that it has that curvy S shape to
it, as though it is preparing to lunge out of the bottle. (Pre-
sentation is everything.) After that, a few sprigs of local
bushes are added for effect, and finally the bottle is filled
with homemade whiskey and sealed. It was fascinating to
watch, and when I asked him if he ever handled live snakes
himself he held up his left hand. It was missing the outer
two fingers and part of his palm. With that he handed me
another drink while also giving one to the monkey, "Mr.

Tojo likes to drink," he said. The monkey threw the shot back like a gunslinger in a B western.

At that point Mr. Kamdee asked if I would care to put a few snakes into the bottles, and, repulsive as I found the idea, I could not refuse. They were quite slippery and I was careful to avoid the fangs that could still hold deadly toxins as they slid easily into the bottles in that classic S shape. Every other bottle I filled brought another shot, one for myself and one for the monkey. I must admit at this point that I was mesmerized by the simian's ability to consume and hold his liquor, and while I would never condone giving booze to an animal, it was obviously a way of life for Mr. Tojo long before my arrival. Realizing the monkey was a hardcore alcoholic, I could not help myself. I had to know who the better man was. Game on.

I put down the snake bottles and picked up my shot glass. Tojo grabbed his drinking bowl and looked me in the eye. Together we finished the latest shots simultaneously and Mr. Kamdee, sensing that an epic competition might be in the works, quickly filled both for us again. Eye to eye, face to face, Tojo and I downed several more drinks, each of us mimicking the motions of the other like two sides of a mirror. Just as I was thinking of throwing in the towel, Tojo began to lean, slowly, ever so slowly, eyes narrowing and teeth grinning, he fell over, hit the ground, and bounced slightly like those slow-motion shots in a Sam Peckinpah western. I should have been embarrassed by my elation at vanquishing a six-pound monkey, but I was not. It felt great. At least now his butt faced the wall as he began to snore like a power saw. The last thing I remember was raising a toast to him and thinking, "Man, that monkey could drink!"

I awoke in the early darkness, head throbbing, to see a grinning set of teeth inches away from my face. If Mr. Tojo was asking for a rematch I was not answering the bell. At that moment I hated the monkey because he was smiling, and therefore could not possibly hurt as badly as I did. Then, in the distance, the hum of an engine came to me from the water and Kamdee helped me to my feet, quietly laughing at the free entertainment I had provided him all afternoon.

He walked me down the bamboo walkway, holding my arm and telling me that I had been a great help to him and should return sometime. He got me into the boat and put my bag next to me, and as we pushed off into the current I could see the bright white of many oversized teeth smiling at me through the bushes. I dozed on and off as we headed south on the Mekong, and only after an hour did I think of looking in my bag to make sure I had everything.

Inside there were two bottles of cobra whiskey and my wallet was lite by $20.

Today, a bottle of cobra whiskey holds a place of honor among the collectables in my television room. My wife threatens to toss it out almost daily, visitors find it disgusting…and my dog growls whenever she notices it.

PART TWO

Discoveries
and Revelations

Jordan's bull

Jordan's Bull

HIPPOS SURFACED WITH WIGGLING EARS AS THE RIVER MAN poled our dhow past the submerged herd. We were both tense, expecting a bluff charge, while only feet away white pelicans with long golden beaks floated in the shallows casually scooping minnows in their great fleshy pouches. On the opposite shore, the grass huts of the Fulani glowed like fiery tumbleweeds in the hazy sunrise as bare-breasted women pounded their dirty wash on river rocks.

At this bend of Mali's Niger River, the lethargic water resembles dark-roasted coffee as it slowly meanders on toward the fabled city of Timbuktu. I was in old spear-and-loincloth Africa to chase the end of an era with my camera.

The Fulani, hereditary nomads of North Africa, had driven over 1,000 head of their cattle onto a small island to graze for a few days and, as is their custom, they had surrounded them with their traditional grass huts. Fulani move about like the wind; they and those like them are vanishing from the African continent.

My dhow was piled with bunches of bananas, gifts of a delicacy hard to come by in such a remote place. I knew from experience that when they saw me coming, the village children would swarm me on the beach, looking for treats.

While passing out the fruit I noticed one little boy sitting by himself, scooping mud from the river. He was fashioning curious animals out of the mud and laying them on a rock in the sand to bake in the sun. They struck me as wonderfully realistic from the hands of one so young. He worked with an intense concentration and the sureness of an instinctive artist that drew me to him. When I approached to tell him how much I liked his animals he did not speak or acknowledge me in any way so I dropped off a banana, left him to his work, and walked up the bank to the village.

There, in front of a grass hut, I was warmly greeted by the village headman named Able, who noting my interest in the boy, told me his name was Jordan. "Like the river in the Bible," he said. Able took both my hands in his and held my gaze as if searching for something in my face or demeanor until he finally added as a matter of fact, "He does not speak. He is touched by God." He then asked me to sit with him and take tea.

While Western medicine has unpronounceable names and diagnoses for various mental states, it has been my experience that in many remote cultures, people like Jordan often come with the title of "Touched by God." In my own country such a child would probably be on a regimen of medications, therapy, or even confined to a "facility" to alter their behavior, but in rural Africa, people like Jordan are believed to exist on an alternate plane and are considered a liaison to the spirit world. Their condition is accepted as a gift to the village and they are often the people who become shamans or healers, commanding both power and respect. In rural Africa there is no mental illness, only spirits, both evil and good.

I drank the obligatory welcome of tea and made small talk as custom demanded, but could not take my eyes off the young boy at the waters' edge. I asked Able if God ever spoke to Jordan or through him and his answer was only an enigmatic smile as he topped off my teacup. I knew that any further questions could only result in a conversation beyond my comprehension because to this man the physical and spirit worlds are intermingled and I am still a long way from being able to claim the same.

With Able's blessing, I wandered into the vast cattle herd to take my photos while clouds of grasshoppers fled my shadow. Men filled calabash gourds with the morning milk then handed them off to young boys who carried the nectar back to the village. The women were busy ferrying goatskin bags of water to the herders. The air was full of bees swollen with pollen and the panoramic sky emphasized the vastness of the African plain. It was a travelers' day when the voices of nature became an aria and the only mechanical sound was that of my shutter capturing limitless beauty. Wood fire smoke mingled with the stench of a thousand feral longhorns when I felt a slight tug on my pant leg. I looked down just as Jordan slipped his hand into mine. I had not heard him coming and he had not said a word. Together we stood surrounded by baying cattle, taking in the moment. He was eating the banana.

I began to walk slowly and Jordan kept my pace, his hand swallowed by my own. As we passed them, people stopped working and stood at an informal attention. I thought at first that they were simply offering a respectful welcome to a visitor but as we continued, I realized it had nothing to do with me. They had stopped their work to acknowledge Jordan as he passed by, but it was more than that.

Travelers are often captured by a vortex beyond their comprehension. Remote journeys can sometimes be disorienting to the point of the wanderer asking themselves, "What just happened?" For many, attaining such a moment is the very reason for traveling. My reasons are built on a history of such events that always seem to find me while in Africa. It is a land steeped in animism, and marinated in voodoo; a land of myth, legend, and ceremony where there is no horizon between the material and spiritual worlds and, by keeping an open mind, I have often found myself treading an edge between the two.

At first, the sound was almost imperceptible from the constant breeze pushed along by the river, but it grew in intensity and volume until I could discern a harmonious chant. It was a traditional chant, the likes of which I have heard countless times in Africa, and yet it was its own. Rather than a narration followed by a chorus it was a constant mantra of the entire village emanating from their souls more than their lungs. It was a sound as old as the earth, a sound that held both agony and ecstasy. It was a sound I felt as much as heard. We were surrounded by the entire village, on their feet, chanting.

It was melodious and calming while suggesting an underlying current of power that held me in a firm grip. I floated in the moment, an organic piece of ancient Africa swept along in its mystery and pageantry. I was no longer a visitor but an integral part of the village and I took in a panorama of the entire scene, hundreds of heads and shoulders interspersed throughout the vast cattle herd, all turned inward toward Jordan, who still held my hand. His head was now tilted skyward, his eyes were closed, and he showed a tiny smile as he wiped banana from his chin.

Was this happening because the village holy man had left his trance to walk among them, or was I, this rare visitor, just an excuse for a spontaneous celebration? I had no idea what was taking place and I really did not care; I only wanted the moment to continue. Jordan was in another place or perhaps he had summoned another place to our here and now and something inside at that moment told me he was indeed, touched by God. Whatever was happening was African, and could never be understood by a non-African, and that was enough for me to know. I just let the chant envelope me.

Jordan began to walk, this time leading me by the hand. The people parted as we passed them but continued their grand chorus. Time had slowed, sound intensified, colors glowed with brilliance, and I held the most sublime sense of belonging that has eluded me most times since. I remember herons flying overhead and egrets by the waterside and thinking how the emerald body of a dead cicada was the most brilliant green I had ever seen. The world had become intense. I was in my body but felt out of it being carried along by the wonderful melody. Hours may have passed but I am sure it was only minutes before I found myself back at Able's hut.

Jordan let go of my hand and returned to the riverside and his clay animals without ever having said a word. I do not remember the chanting coming to an end but suddenly all I heard was silence and when I looked about, people were returning to work tending the cattle. I felt elated yet unsure, as if exiting a dream. Able's face carried a knowing smile that made me wonder if other visitors had had such a day as mine.

It was late afternoon and the golden sky was turning crimson as the African sun submerged into the black water. People became silhouettes as Able walked me to the rivers' edge where the river man waited for my return. We exchanged no words because none were sufficient. Our mutual silence was enough validation that something extraordinary had taken place. As I walked past Jordan he rose and pressed something into my hand, folding my fingers around it with great solemnity. He did not speak and made no eye contact. He simply returned to his place by the water and his clay animals. His gift was small, hard, and cool in my hand and I held it there, not looking at it until we reached the center of the river. It was a tiny clay bull, just like those that had surrounded us all day, Paleolithic in simplicity, pregnant with symbolism.

I did not watch for hippos during our return crossing or notice the ethereal beauty of the West African sunset. I could only stare at the tiny figure in my palm, running my fingers over it and reliving the day in my soul. I did no analysis nor did I yearn for answers. In truth, I often prefer the what-if to what is, and this was one of those times. I wanted only the day as it was, now a memory, but one that I could recall whenever I wished by the tiny clay bull I now held in my hand. Since that day Jordan's bull has become both talisman and artifact, and perhaps, even a relic.

Later, at a café in Timbuktu, I met two people who had both preceded me to the island. Both had taken notice of the silent boy by the water. They both told me he had not reacted to them in any way and the people had been friendly but had not sung or chanted. I could drive myself crazy with speculation of "Why me?" so I chose to go with "Why not me?"

Whether Jordan was "Touched by God" or simply a mute little boy, he held great face among his people and for his own reasons, took me into an unexplainable afternoon that has affected and elevated my life in the years that followed.

I am sure the world is full of Jordans, mostly overlooked or even ignored, walking among us, visible only to those with open minds and hearts. Maybe all it takes to have the kind of day a traveler prays for is to give a boy a banana.

From the Ashes

THE SMOKE OF WOOD FIRES DULLS THE SUNRISE, SILHOUETT-ing the spires of Angkor Wat as if in an Impressionist painting, and as the sun climbs, I watch their hazy shadow retreat from my feet like an ebbing tide.

From cracks between stones on the moat a lone cicada keeps up its tattoo, oblivious to the fact that it is long past dawn, while across the road, a thro player from Phum Chom Rika, the nearby village of land-mine victims, coaxes a soulful melody from the lone string on his instrument. Monkeys, the praetorian guard of every temple, have started their endless chatter, announcing that the jungle is rousing from sleep.

I turn to watch a screeching flight of wild parrots skim the water that rings these temples; these gorgeous temples, the soul of the Khmer nation. This land radiates peace and makes an ironic backdrop for the tale of horror I have come to record.

I see Pan approaching, fingering his prayer beads, his saffron robes seemingly ablaze in the yellow mist. He walks as though he is not really there, feet barely touching the ground, a saint incarnate to the world at large, but, in his own eyes, a simple, humble monk. His body is bent from time and suffering, having lived through and seen more than anyone should, and I know through mutual

Pan, the survivor

friends, he wishes nothing more than to spend his remaining time in secluded meditation, but upon hearing of my book project, he readily agreed to speak with me in the hopes that no one should have to relive what he has.

Pan is a Theravada monk, one of about 350,000 throughout Cambodia prior to the Khmer Rouge, and now one of about 300 to have outlived their regime. Besides surviving personal atrocities, he bears the weight of trying to re-establish a religious order dragged to the brink of extinction under a barbaric reign.

Theravada means "Teaching of the Elders." It is one of three main branches of Buddhism that originated in northern India and lower Nepal in the sixth century b.c., spreading rapidly throughout Southeast Asia until it was introduced to Cambodia in the 13th century via monks from Sri Lanka. It is a personal religion that worships no deity but rather teaches self-control in order to release all attachment to the material world and achieve personal enlightenment. Most Khmer men spend time as a novice before deciding to permanently don the saffron robes or return to a secular life. For many, the robes are the only escape from a life of dire poverty and hope for at least a minimal education. For Pan, it was a calling that put him in the eye of the storm.

The reign of the Khmer Rouge has been likened to a shark attack, increasing in speed and fury, feeding upon its own momentum as more and more blood is spilled. In the headlong rush to turn Cambodia into a submissive, agrarian, socialist state, it was the Buddhist monks who bore the brunt of the assault. Why do the innocent always suffer the most? Perhaps it is a purification rite on their trail to sainthood.

Their modest education made the monks a threat to the beast and since they do not work in the traditional sense of the word, they became an easy target, publicly declared useless and a drain on society to be removed. It has always been easy to kill people who do not fight back.

Pan sits next to me on the stone railing of the Angkor moat bridge, lightly as a sparrow and unrolls an oilcloth from the folds of his robes. The cicada has ceased its chant and retreated from the gathering crowd. Inside the cloth is a shiny bowl; his rice bowl he says.

He runs his finger around the rim and in a matter of fact voice says that it is the top of his own brother's skull, killed by the Khmer Rouge. In true Buddhist fashion, he has kept it as a daily reminder of his own frailty and impermanence, and it is his way of beginning his story of survival. He stares at his dangling sandaled feet, too short to reach the ground, kicking them out like a child on a swing as he speaks. There is no self-pity or even regret in his voice.

His story begins with the first night, when he was still a novice, lighting candles around the monastery when the door burst open and everyone was herded outdoors at gunpoint. There was no panic at first, only confusion. Outside, in a huddled mass, the Abbott and all elders were singled out and summarily shot with a single bullet to the back of the head. By now, the attendant nuns were being stripped by the soldiers, intent on a long night of debauchery. Cries and whimpers began to emanate from the victims, betraying those not sufficiently spiritual to take such actions in their stride.

Next he tells me several monks were hung in the trees by their thumbs with small fires built beneath them, not enough to kill, but just large enough to singe the skin. According to Pan, an elderly monk named Non thanked his tormentors for their actions. One of the nuns, who was now hysterical, was stripped, held down, and a monk was made to kneel between her knees. A pistol was put to his head and he was ordered to copulate with her in front of all present. When he refused, a single shot rang out to the applause and cheers of the "soldiers" splattering the hysterical nun with blood and brain matter, and another monk was brought forward. According to Pan, this went on for quite a while, until several monks had done the deed, while several more had died in refusing. The nun, covered with victim's blood and now shaking in silent fear, was left staked to the ground to die slowly.

I search his face at this point for some sign, some emotional reaction, but see only tranquility. His roadmap face is a spider web of creases but his eyes burn bright. I pray his religious advancement had brought him true peace and that he is not simply numb in relating such unspeakable events. He returns my stare with a slight smile and says, "Tell this story once so it might never be told a second time." His courage is beyond my comprehension and while he does not cry, my tears flow freely as I make a silent vow to never forget.

We begin to walk into the main courtyard of Angkor and though surrounded by thousands of tourists, I hear only Pan as he continues in his soft voice.

He was sent to the countryside and made to rip up railroad tracks, brutally physical work under an unforgiving sun while enduring nonstop blows from the fists and whips of his overseers. Soon, near starvation, and with only putrid river water to drink, he was near death, the final plan for him from the beginning. In the end, his involuntary will to live overcame his faith in karma as he crawled away one night, into the jungle, and there, lost all track of time.

Pan continues slowly until a beautiful yellow butterfly zigs by us in its kamikaze flight plan. His conversation trails away to a whisper as I see his eyes following the creature that adds a smile to his face. In that second, he is totally immersed in the butterfly and his true self comes forth. Pan occupies a separate reality, a spiritual place I can only hope to reach one day. To him it is all karma, and all that surrounds him now is but Maya, an illusion to wander through until he reaches true enlightenment. It is this detachment that allows him to continue his story.

He was not sure how long he stayed in the jungle, but once there he found others like himself, survivors, all with an unspeakable story, all wishing to live. Everyone had a talent; some could fish, others snared small animals. Pan knew a lot about medicinal plants and so became a gypsy doctor, moving every few days, avoiding roads and villages, helping the more needy for a handful of rice, defying the odds as a refugee in his own land; never revealing who or what he was.

Sleep was taken in the branches of trees or buried under piles of leaves; he caught fish bare-handed, eating them raw, and with time suspended, he soon became feral, avoiding those who might betray him. Instincts were honed to equality with the creatures of the forest around him as he surrendered to being one of its denizens.

One day, while foraging near a village, he spotted a saffron robe and, not believing his eyes, knew he had to talk with this brother. Pan could not remember the last time he spoke and at first the words choked in his mouth. The startled monk thought he was being attacked by a wild animal, and in fact, that is just what Pan had become.

The Khmer Rouge were gone but the damage had been done. Pan listened to the monk's litany of atrocities all day as humanity flowed slowly back into his body. At the end of the monk's tale, he fell asleep, and the next morning, he woke up under a roof, on a cot, for the first time in months, if not years.

When he revealed his identity, he was called to the capitol of Phnom Penh where he was received as a revered elder and met a delegation of Theravada monks from

Vietnam who had come to help re-establish the religion. Only then did he realize the extent of the genocide, the monasteries destroyed, the sacred texts burned, countless brother monks slaughtered, and for the only time in our conversations, I saw a single tear roll down his cheek.

Two subsequent visits with Pan were deliberately kept light-hearted and fun and I learned that he loved shaved ice, and to laugh, but it is more of a sustained giggle that spares no part of his face. His joy in all that surrounds him is like a small child's and though I could not see it, I often felt his aura. This was man; descended into animal, and returned as a saint, for what else could I possibly call him?

When I left Cambodia, Pan was in great demand, traveling around to various monasteries, imparting the old ways, "The Teaching of the Elders" to a new generation of monks who now used the internet, had cellphones and iPads, and ride motorbikes, but this did not seem to bother him in the least. It was karma.

His goal had always been to spend his life in meditation and I am sure that since our time together he has merged with the cosmos. I have allowed myself the fantasy to think he may have been looking over my shoulder as I wrote this and would know that his story had been told, one more time, for the last time.

Today there are close to 60,000 Theravada monks in Cambodia and almost 5,000 monasteries, all because men like Pan refused to give up their faith, and though he would laugh and shake his head at the thought, he is one who made a difference.

Maasai coming to see us

My Maasai
Night

Travel does not always begin with the boarding of an airplane, but rather at the moment one opens the mind to new possibilities. That is why I was quite surprised when the gentleman I had engaged in dinner conversation at a party in Los Angeles told me he was an elder of the Maasai nation, one of Africa's most ancient warrior societies.

Moses was in America to study theology at a local seminary, a contradiction for the traditional Maasai who, as animists, shun Western-style education. When finished, he would be only the sixth Maasai known to receive a Ph.D. Today, years later, besides having created a foundation that drills water wells and builds schools, he has become an executive at World Vision.

After a year of invitations, my wife and I found ourselves on a hot, dusty, African savannah, and the culture shock was complete when I saw Moses, normally clad in blue jeans and a blazer, in his brilliant red shuka, (Maasai robe) with a long spear. The only familiar connection was his brilliant smile as I saw my old friend for the first time in his natural state; a man of power and respect, within his own element.

We spent that first afternoon walking through his valley while Moses spun tales of growing up with wild animals for companions, and not hearing a mechanical sound until he was almost ten years old. Two young warriors followed us carrying their spears. I did not take much notice of this until Moses pointed at a tree and there, in the crook of a large branch, I saw a leopard watching us with intense curiosity. Moses told me there were many leopards about and spoke of how the Maasai feared them more than lions. It seems a lion will make a kill and drag it away to eat it while a leopard will kill every living thing in sight before settling down for a meal. I spent the rest of our walk look-ing back over my shoulder.

The Maasai have a connection to the earth that is beyond the comprehension of those of us who dwell in cities; it is their mother and the cradle of their ancestors. The literature and oral histories of Judeo-Christianity have taught their followers that a person's essence, or soul "goes to heaven," an unseen place somewhere away from the earth, as the body disappears. Indigenous societies in Africa have no such concept. They believe their ancestors sleep in the ground below their feet and they are only separated by a few inches of dirt. This creates a very per-sonal connection through ceremony. While Westerners do not talk directly to their ancestors, many Africans do.

The Maasai also have little concept of time, and why should they? Nature is their clock, and as nomads, they wander like the wind. However, when they occasionally run afoul of the laws of the land because of marks on paper they do not always understand, and are put in jails, they usually die, unable to imagine ever being free again.

They live accordingly as stewards of the earth. Moses told us how to track an animal, how to read its scat, and know its sex by the depth of its print in the dirt. He showed us how to follow a trail by the bend of a leaf, and I realized that while in Africa, he occupied a separate reality than I did, and I marveled at how he transitioned from one to the other with ease.

He spoke of how as traditional nomads, he was never sure where his family would be whenever he returned to Africa. He would simply go to the last place their village existed and wander until he found them. I asked how the Maasai navigate in the bush and Moses just smiled and said, "A Maasai may not always know where he is, but he is never lost." He was the first person I had ever met who was at home wherever he was.

When we returned to the village, he invited us inside his hut and became very serious, asking if we wanted to know about hunting lions. Lion hunting has long been central to Maasai culture. In olden days, before a Maasai boy could be considered a man, he had to participate in a lion hunt using only a spear and buffalo hide shield. The first lion hunt was the paramount point in the life of a Maasai youth, and nothing he did for the rest of his life would equal its importance.

Even though this practice was outlawed by the Kenyan government long ago, the Maasai still practice it covertly, and Moses was being unusually candid by his willingness to share such intimate information.

He stared into the fire for a long time before speaking, and I knew this story would be a rare gift to me as a friend. The word "friend" carries greater meaning to the Maasai, much more than in Western society. To them it is more like being a brother, and when Moses applied it to me, it touched my soul.

Moses was about 13 when he was picked for his first lion hunt, determined to prove himself and gain great face, but he admitted to such fear that he could not sleep the night before the hunt. On the actual morning, while his face was being painted as a warrior for the first time, he felt everyone could hear his heart pounding, and was sure all would notice the spear shaking in his hand. As the warriors gathered in the morning mist, his knees almost buckled. He was told to lead the way into the bush.

The Maasai hunt a lion by forming a circle around it and then slowly walk forward, tightening that circle. Eventually the lion will feel cornered and spring at one man who is supposed to drop to the ground, cover himself with his shield, and hope his fellow warriors kill the lion before it kills him. It is an archaic and honored part of their culture. On that day, Moses took his place in the circle, facing one of the top predators of the animal world with only a spear.

He paused briefly as though the words were hard to come by and I took the moment to imagine myself in his position, but, I could not.

Suddenly, and with a great flare, Moses reached down and pulled up his shuka, revealing a long jagged scar running for several inches along his lower leg. He stared at the scar for several seconds before saying in a very soft voice, "From my first lion hunt!"

I was stunned and blurted out, "The lion did that to you?"

Moses looked me square in the eye and said, "No, I was so scared I speared myself in the leg, and the lion got away!" and with that he threw his head back and laughed. To this day, Moses has never killed a lion, but he certainly ambushed me. I should add here that storytelling is a much-honored Maasai talent.

As rare guests we dined on goat that evening while a chorus of cicadas announced the coming of the African night, and I pondered how my Western girth would fit inside one of their tiny huts whose sleeping compartments resemble those of a working man's hotel in Tokyo, much like sliding into a beehive.

When I expressed this concern to Moses he pointed just outside the acacia bush wall that surrounds the village where two of his nephews were wrestling with a nylon tent. He was way ahead of me.

Grateful as I was for this comfort, I was terrified by the thought of sleeping outside the thorn wall with the image of a leopard dragging my bloody carcass into a tree to munch on at a later date.

Noting my apprehension, Moses told us that if the leopard should come, we need only yell and a dozen warriors would come running with spears, then he put his hand on my shoulder and said with gravity not to worry as the leopard would not like our smell, and with that he walked off, secure in his pronouncement. His words alone carried enough comfort for us to sleep outside.

No sooner were Irene and I in the tent than most of the village surrounded us, pulling the zipper up and down while running their hands over the strange new sensation of nylon. Most of them had never seen a tent before, and they called it a "fast hut."

A full moon was rising over the tree line, turning the silhouettes of our curious visitors into a shadow-puppet show crawling on our tent walls. Surreal patterns glided over the nylon as tiny fingers poked and prodded and old hands ran up and down. After a few minutes we became concerned about being such an oddity, having no wish to offend our guests by disrupting village life, and that is just what we were doing. At first we stayed inside hoping to minimize our impact, but this only fed the people's curiosity, and rather than winding down, more and more people were arriving. I finally stepped outside to see just how many there were.

Perhaps a dozen people surrounded the tent while a line of Maasai snaked through the forest and disappeared far down into the valley. The jungle telegraph was

humming that night. It looked as though the entire valley was migrating toward our "fast hut." Hundreds of red
shukas, turned purple by the moonlight, ambled up the
hill like so many giant chess pieces, and that sight is now
forever imbedded in my memory.

Irene stepped outside to greet our visitors. Most shook
our hands while others simply wanted to touch us. For
some, we would be the only outsiders they would ever
see. No one spoke and there was no need for words. In
that magical evening we were all simply people, coming
together to meet each other for the first and only time, frozen by a human touch that instantly passed into memory.

I have no idea how long we stood there, but such a
gift encounter turned the event into an endless night.
There would be no sleep and we did not care. No festival,
ceremony, or dance, could have been more entertaining
or enlightened us more. All future days should strive to
approximate this one.

As I said earlier, despite having no written language, the
Maasai have become master storytellers. Stories quickly
become both history and legend and tend to grow with
each telling as they take on the flavor of the individual
narrator.

I like to think that on that evening we became one of
their stories.

My Mexican Bus

WE ALL HAVE A SPECIAL PLACE FOR SOLACE AND INTROSPEC-
tion; mine is a southbound bus in Baja Mexico.

I only take this ride once a year to visit friends, but
it has become both a pilgrimage and a ritual that occupies my thoughts for a far greater time. I seem to have an
inbred need for this repetitive ride that would not have
the same value should I do it more often. For me, the
journey has always been as important as the destination,
but in this case, they are both the same.

It begins in the Tijuana bus terminal, an aging, cavernous building and a time portal for my entree to old Mexico.
When I step through those doors I have entered another
era as well as a place. The concrete-and-glass blockhouse
is a utilitarian monument to 1950's Mexican architecture
and a reminder of how slowly time passes here. Inside,
the smell of tortillas and mole mingles with the aroma of
ammonia on linoleum floors. A feeling washes over me
that does not translate easily into words, a feeling finely
honed and nuanced over many years, somewhere between
coming home and simple tranquility.

I pay my respects at the shrine to the Virgin of Guadalupe, whose statue stands a tearful guard next to the
entrance to the public toilet. I drop a two-peso coin into
the pay slot that lets me revolve the steel turnstile and open

65

The overnight bus

the door marked "Caballeros" over the grinning stencil of a mustachioed man giving me a thumbs up. Inside, I am pleasantly surprised to find flush toilets complete with paper but know they will probably be the last of their kind until I reach my final destination.

Outside in the main hall I walk past the "cambio" money exchange that has never been open in my presence, and then wait while the young girl behind the counter writes out my ticket by hand on a yellow legal pad with a dull pencil as she snaps her gum loudly. I am distracted by her amply filled T-shirt that reads, "Hecho en Mexico."

Tijuana is an open city with no taxes and it is here that the braceros and agriculturos of the south come to stock up on the trappings of modern society only recently available from the large new discount stores that line the border. The waiting hall is full of people lugging big screen TVs and assorted appliances on those tiny folding luggage rollers. One ancient grandmother has three crowded shopping bags on each arm that cause her to roll like a camel as she walks. I watch a mother wrap her children in blankets on the cold steel chairs and try to make out what the PA announcement is saying, but it is mostly garbled static.

With my fellow passengers, I walk through the metal detector that beeps loudly at each of us but fails to gain the attention of the bored-looking security guard. The folding knife I forgot to take out of my pocket will ride with me tonight.

Outside, standing in line to board, the tiny grandmother clutching a canvas bag in front of me is startled when I greet her in Spanish. She is so wide that it is an effort to board, but once in her seat, she pats the one next to her when I climb on. She offers me a bite of her churro that I politely decline, then instinctively clutches my hand as the bus lurches from its stall. Her lips are moving below closed eyes and I think she is saying the Lord's Prayer. She

is a child of the old world and clearly afraid of the journey ahead in this gigantic mechanized machine. She has
probably left the desert for the first time to visit a son or
daughter and now must return. Her weathered face is a
definitive map of the Mexican people; not Hispanic, nor
Spanish, or even Mestizo, but Mexican; a distinction often
overlooked by racial generalization. I assure her in Spanish
that all will be well and she nervously compliments me on
my pronunciation.

Baja is not like mainland Mexico. It is older and set
in its ways. On the world scale it is a tiny peninsula, but
its deserts rival any on Earth and its jagged mountains
appear shaped by an angry God, while tucked into its most
remote corners are a people whose mode of living has not
changed in centuries. They are the same people whose
ancestors turned back armored Spanish conquistadors
with bows and arrows. Away from Highway One, horses
and burros are the main mode of transport and doors of
mud houses remain unlocked because there is no crime
among neighbors. Cattle wander the highways with faces
full of prickly Cholla cactus and cougars and wolves roam
in numbers across a vast lunar landscape. It is a separate
reality from my own life and part of its allure is to realize
that an imaginary line on a map is all it takes to divide
such diverse cultures.

The noisy diesel coughs and sputters to life and we
begin to inch our way past the gaudy neon and gridlocked
traffic that is the Tijuana night. From my perch high above
them I wonder about the lives in the countless cars below
me thinking any one of them could have been my own.
What if I had been born here? How would my life be
different?

A big difference is obvious when our route takes us
past the high concrete wall that forms part of the border.
It is covered with graffiti and seems eerily similar to one

that used to stand in Berlin. While people are not being shot for crossing this wall it still makes me think about a world where we need no barriers to separate us from our neighbors.

As we leave the city behind, grandmother releases my hand and with a timid smile of apology, falls asleep with her head on my shoulder. She is going home now and is happy. A pearl-white smiling moon slides from behind traveling clouds to reveal iridescent rolling surf just before the highway turns inland on the way to Ensenada.

In the silent cloak of night, Mexico has always been more real to me. In this predominately Catholic land, organized religion has merged with peasant superstition to create a belief system all its own, especially in the high mountains and remote desserts where I prefer to travel. This is the land of the brujo, witches, spirits, and demons, a land where people pray equally to Jesus in church and to syncretic images of Santeria in mud shacks. I have spent too much time in this place to dismiss anything metaphysical and recall a midnight encounter in a coffee shop when a stranger swathed in black warned me of the full moon and then disappeared into a brightly lit and vacant street. I have yet to meet anyone in Baja who is not related to, or had an encounter with a witch of some sort. They are ubiquitous in Baja.

South of Ensenada, we climb into the mountains of San Pedro de Martir. The temperature has fallen and I pull a fleece from my bag as the repetitive hum of the tires and familiar back and forth swaying on the switchbacked road triggers more memories.

Guillermo was on the lead horse when it reared up, and without any commands, trampled a rattlesnake to death. Its patterned skin eventually became a somewhat mutilated hat band. Later that day, while returning from a cave painted 6,000 years ago by the Cochimi people;

we stopped at a rancho for beans and rice. I noticed what appeared to be a human skull on a shelf in the adobe. When I turned to ask the old patron about it, his face appeared weirdly contorted and I suddenly felt dizzy. The moment passed, and when I looked again, the skull was a chunk of obsidian and the old man was smiling benignly. That revelatory moment ended any more questions on my part. Some things are just not meant to be understood.

The hours pass while my thoughts are elsewhere. Night in a foreign land is when I rethink my own life; what I should have done differently, what I can do better. What will I do next? The bus is silent except for random snoring and the hushed conversation between the middle-aged driver and his young girlfriend, seated on the aisle floor next to him. We stop on an isolated piece of road where towering cactus stand like night sentinels in our headlights. The cargo door opens and a gentleman and young lady emerge to trade places with the driver and his friend, both girls giggling as they switch. Our new driver, refreshed in more ways than one, takes over.

I return to the night and when the first purple streak of dawn slashes the sky we leave Highway One for the service road into Guerro Negro, gateway to Scammon's Lagoon. On the sides of the road we begin to see platforms topping telephone poles for the osprey to nest on and avoid electrocution. On the beach side we roll past the enormous skeleton of a gray whale that announces this village as a major whale-watching destination.

Behind the bus station, the ever-present Virgin of Guadalupe, haloed by blinking Christmas lights, watches over the parking lot with outstretched hands. A faint whiff of marijuana comes to my nose and stepping inside, two ancient and gaunt vaqueros in straw cowboy hats are drinking coffee and passing a hand rolled smoke. I buy a cold empanada so stale I toss it to a stray dog after one bite.

Because it is close to the ocean, it is often bitterly cold in Guerro Negro at night. This evening I watch my breath rise in hazy clouds to disappear in the breeze. Above me, the Big Dipper sits low in the sky, the end of its handle pointing the way home for when I return. As we leave to continue south, the morning light begins to crawl over the horizon, mingling land and sky that slowly separates into a new day.

An hour's ride south, the desert floor widens and the road disappears into a cottony ground fog. The top of a distant volcano pokes through it and gigantic Cordon cactus slide in and out of sight in the haze, their upturned arms saluting as we roll past, a vast silent army, icons of the land. We have reached the edge of the Vizcaino biosphere, five million hectares of protected wilderness that covers a quarter of the Baja Peninsula. Suddenly, distant shadows become a herd of wild burros that cause us to brake hard enough to wake everyone and we laugh as the driver must exit and physically shoo them off the road. Kestrels are hunting insects in the morning haze and the cactus appears to be stretching after the evenings sleep. Everyone crowds to one side and cell phones are snapping photos. The quiet night is gone. Across from me, a man in silver-tipped cowboy boots, draws a long pull from a pocket flask then slumps back in his seat, his Stetson tilted low over his eyes.

The fog parts like a curtain and we pass low flat mesas full of sandstone caves carved by the eons. I know if I were to explore them I would find artifacts that hold stories from centuries ago. East of the mesas, rolling flat lands give rise to the Tres Virgines, three active volcanoes, named for the inhabitants of an old folk tale. They sit in a perfect row, descending in height from the one nearest the highway, all mighty vents from the lungs of the planet. Archeologists have speculated that when they last awoke, tens of thousands of years ago, they spewed molten lava up to 100 miles, all the way to the Pacific Ocean, from whose tidal waters on a clear day you can see the hazy outline of the tallest volcano.

Just north of San Ignacio we stop for a military checkpoint where a cardboard soldier holds a sign warning against drugs. An officer with a clipboard climbs into the bus and struts up and down the center aisle, not really looking for anything; more an act of machismo than a search. Outside a sniffer dog scratches at the baggage compartment and after an amused soldier looks inside we are waved on.

People are moving about the bus, stiff and sore after the long night. The driver puts a movie on the overhead screens and cranks the volume up to rock concert level. It is *Snakes on a Plane* starring Samuel L. Jackson, a very bad B movie that makes me realize that a good movie is not about to play on a public bus in the rural desserts of Mexico.

We round a hairpin turn and from the tiny valley below us, the adobe-tiled roofs of San Ignacio come into view through the date palms. It is a tired and sun-worn village whose main industry is cement bricks and whose people appear to live in slow motion. The town sits astride an impossibly beautiful river full of egrets and herons that contribute to the town's casual aura. Two hours to the west, gray whales have migrated into the lagoon of the same name for centuries.

We pull into the dirt parking lot and I spot Jorge leaning against his van, waiting for me even though we are three hours late. He has one cowboy boot on the bumper above a "Jesus loves you" decal and his arm rests on the bullhorns mounted on the hood. He still wears the aviator shades I gave him two years ago. It is stifling hot under a van Gogh sun.

A stray dog barks at a swirling dust devil and I stare up at the familiar sign over the bus office.

I smile as I read, "Bienvenido a San Ignacio."

I am back in Mexico.

Bingwen

A Life
Not Chosen

I WATCHED THE OLD MAN FOR ABOUT AN HOUR BEFORE I approached him. He sat on a dirty blanket on the street corner, bent like a sextant with age, rats scuttling in the gutter below his feet. That was his spot; I had seen so many like him throughout China: Those without status who survive by their wits.

His clothes were tattered and his four-cornered hat identified him as a Uyghur, one of the displaced Eastern European Muslims trapped on the wrong side of a line on a map. China has declared Xinxiang province to be a "Uyghur Autonomous Area," but that is only lip service to a minority that is scorned by the ruling Han majority. The Uyghur are Chinese on paper only.

I watched him work with infinite care, carving with a tiny penknife. He was oblivious to the uninterested masses passing him by, focused only on his work. No one stopped to buy or even look at his wares; delicate wooden combs, spoons, and whimsical creatures. He was an artist by any reasonable standards, but his birth status had relegated him to the streets. His leathery skin looked like an aerial map of old dried riverbeds, and his whippet-thin arms ended in gnarled hands bulging with purple veins. They were craftsman's hands that liberated beauty from old blocks of wood. In another time and place, he might have been a great sculptor, but in today's China, he was but one of those who do not officially exist. He was the kind of person I seek to have a conversation.

In rural China, Westerners are a curiosity, especially those of us who stand over six feet tall and weigh 200 pounds, so my approach brought with it a crowd, and crowds always bring the police. I sat on his blanket, fingering his works, while he cocked his head studying this strange foreigner who was giving him face by sitting near him. Within a minute we were surrounded by a pushing mass of onlookers including two young policemen who were obviously out of their league in dealing with such a situation. They seemed as curious about me as I was about the old man.

He spoke halting English with a strange accent, so, intrigued, I invited him to join me in a local tea house, I knew that under normal circumstances he would not be allowed to enter. But the Chinese get jittery in the presence of Westerners, especially those with cameras, and I suspected they would not challenge me if he entered as my guest.

All heads turned and eyes stared as we took seats on the patio, while necks craned to hear the strange language being exchanged between this unlikely pair. The waiter served my tea but placed the pot on the table without pouring the old man's, so I picked it up and made a show of pouring his, as a gasp of astonishment spread across the tables. Then to counter the local arrogance, I called the waiter back and ordered two bagels, knowing them to be a Uyghur favorite, and put them in front of the old man while the waiter glared. The two young police just stood blankly staring, hoping no trouble would start. I am sure they were terrified of something happening, and they would not know how to react.

The old gentleman tore into the bagels with relish and told me his name was Bingwen, which translate roughly to someone having wisdom. Then, eyeing the room about us, he asked why I wanted to talk to him. I told him his story just might be one of those lost epics that fall through the cracks of society, lost forever except for chance encounters. I told him I chase around the world looking for stories like that. My answer made him smile and he shifted in his seat, trying to decide if I was worth talking to, or maybe a government plant sent to trip him up somehow.

He grew silent, and briefly went elsewhere while his body remained. Then he looked up slowly and held my gaze. "If you want to know, I will tell you," he said, "but it was so long ago." He delivered that last line with such world weariness that I felt he was finally casting off a burden.

He said that his father had been one of the last great merchants of the northern Silk Road camel caravans out of Kashgar, and that while quite young he had traveled with his father for the first time, when bandits attacked in the mountains of Afghanistan at a caravanserai on a moonless night. They killed everyone, except Bingwen, who smeared himself with blood and hid under a dead camel until the carnage and looting was over. Now, a homeless orphan, alone for the first time, he made his way to Kabul in a journey worthy of a Kipling novel, begging for food and sleeping on the streets amid packs of roving feral dogs.

He had been a street urchin until a furnituremaker took pity on him and allowed him to sweep out his shop at night in exchange for a little food and a blanket to sleep on. It was in that tiny shop, immersed in the smell of wood, that his muse found him. He knew immediately that wood was his destined medium just as stone had been Michelangelo's, and paint had been Leonardo's. The carving tools felt like extensions of his hands, and he instinctively knew what to do with them. One night, using a cast-off block, and with no training whatsoever, he worked through dawn, answering a call from deep within himself. For him, carving wood was the same as prayer. In the morning he astonished his master with a beautifully rendered horse, rearing on its hind legs, perfectly balanced, anatomically correct in every detail. When asked how he did it he just stared at his hands, wondering the same question himself. He had only seen horses in pictures before.

Within a year he had his own studio and a full list of clientele that expanded greatly after the Soviet invasion of 1979. Feeling no allegiance to his imposed home, he was apolitical at first; but grateful that his carvings were popular souvenirs with the Soviet troops who filled the streets of Kabul and who bought everything he could produce. Life was not bad under the Soviets.

At this point he stopped and I could tell the words were coming hard. I poured him another cup of tea as he began to speak of a young girl who cleaned and cooked for him in exchange for a place to sleep, a kindred spirit, child of the street, just as he had been. One night, three drunken soldiers broke in for a night of debauchery. When he came to her defense, they beat him senseless with camel whips. He awoke the following morning in a pool of blood beside her lifeless body. He stared at her for most of a day, and that night he set fire to his studio and walked off into the hills to find the Mujahideen.

In the purple mountains that cradle Kabul he swore allegiance to a local warlord who sensed a rage in his new fighter that few of his own men possessed. He was there to kill Soviets and he would disappear each night, alone, returning in the morning with proof of his kills, an ear, a finger, an officer's sidearm, driven by the image of the girl in his studio. He was a proficient enough killer to have the Soviets place a price on his head.

One night he attacked the crew of a Soviet tank, who were sitting under their vehicle around a sterno fire. He killed three before the last one managed to slide a bayonet between his ribs as his final act. Bingwen packed the wound with mud made from dirt and his own blood, then crawled into a dry gulley to die. That night was the first time he had noticed the stars since he was a small boy. Their beauty took his pain away and he stared at them, smiling, waiting for the end.

A shepherd found him the next morning, barely alive, and dragged him to his village where the Mujahideen tended him until he was ready to fight again, but something had happened that night under the stars.

Who knows what powers determine our life paths? Certainly, as a child, Bingwen never imagined himself a killer. Our choices can be decided by the toss of a coin, a momentary whim, a sign by the road, or a knife in the gut in a remote desert. Lying under the stars, Bingwen knew that no matter how many soldiers he killed, he could not change the past. It was time to move on.

He left on a moonless night, without provisions or money, AWOL from both sides of the endless war, wandering like a biblical mendicant, unwashed, unshaven, unknown, seeking silent forgiveness from all he met for deeds he dragged around like a stone. His only possession was the small penknife he used to whittle tree branches; his personal meditation.

Perhaps it was divine guidance or just serendipity, that led him to Bamiyan. There he sat in the famous caves with sadhus until they accepted him as one of their own. It had never been his intent to become a hermit, especially a religious one, but his grief was too overwhelming to allow any other life. Living at the foot of a 150-foot-tall stone Buddha, he soaked up Buddhism the way a sponge gathers water.

After months spent in self-reflection, he eventually come to terms with his past, and in time, he left the caves. He felt the need to visit his childhood home, to chase after memories of a life left undone. For a year he wandered the 890 kilometers back to his birth city of Kashgar, China, living off the kindness of those he passed, looking like a wild man with uncut hair and tattered rags. Once there he found that he no longer knew the city. He could not even find the place where he had lived, but while searching for it, he passed a carpentry shop, and the smell of wood called him like a drug, a scent imprinted in his soul.

The owner gave him a small block and he carried it to the park, savoring its feel. There, the memory returning to his fingers, his penknife removed all excess shavings to reveal a beautiful little camel that had been hiding inside. He had not carved in years and he felt his soul beginning to awaken. He carved like a starving man eats until he fell asleep there in the park, at peace with himself and the world for the first time in memory. When he awoke in the morning his carving was gone but there was a note in his pocket with some money, thanking him for the beautiful creature, and asking if he would carve more?

So that was his story that ended in a Kashgar tea house with an American writer. He had reduced his world to a small square blanket and that was all he wanted. He thanked me for the tea and bagels but I could tell he was uneasy in our situation. He had said all he had to say, and now that street corner was his home and wood was his religion and salvation. His creatures were a fantasy world where there was no violence, no war, no rapes, and he was in control of it.

He had come full circle, from a young child to an old man. Perhaps his childhood home was only a few feet from where he now spent his days, but he would never know for sure, nor did he care. He wanted nothing more from life than oblivion within his blocks of wood, and I think I understood that. For many, there may be a fine line between oblivion and Nirvana.

Travel has taught me that he world is full of Bingwens who go unnoticed every day. Everyone has a story worth telling. That is why I start conversations with strangers when I travel, because sometimes, something as simple as tea and a bagel can bring an epic tale in return.

I am probably the only person who has ever heard Bingwen's story, and I still wonder why he chose to tell it to me. Perhaps, I sometimes think, our meeting was just a part of some larger carving.

PART THREE

Adrenalin

The Bin Laden train

Common Ground in the Kasbah

THE CORNER TABLE ON THE PATIO OF THE ARGANA CAFÉ IN the Marrakesh medina was a perfect place to watch the busiest public square in Africa come to life under a blinding sunrise.

Rabat is the capitol of Morocco, and Marrakesh is its heart, but the medina—its center—is an Arabic word that simply means "town," and it is the soul that beats the heart.

Marrakesh is a Berber word that translates roughly to "Land of God." It was founded by the Almoravid dynasty in 1072 and was so powerful a city that until the 20th century all of Morocco was known as the Kingdom of Marrakesh. The Jamaa El Fna Square, in the medina, is a churning cauldron of humanity that only stops long enough each night to catch its breath for the next day. Its name, Jamaa El Fna can be said to mean "Gathering of Trespassers."

At sunrise, merchants and vendors flow in like a slowly creeping tide; umbrellas and awnings sprouting like mushrooms, and all appear like spirits through the blinding light. Snake charmers, rock stars of the square, claim their ground with cheap carpets on which they deposit numerous rubber reptiles to give volume to the handful of living ones they actually possess. Next, they bring out puff adders with lips sewn shut, fierce looking but now benign, followed by cobras so tranquilized they cannot strike, while good old American-style defanged rattlesnakes round out the menagerie. Still the presence of such exotic and normally lethal creatures always draws a paying crowd. More than any other attraction, it is the snake handlers in their pointy yellow shoes, playing their flutes, while a supposedly mesmerized cobra sways to its melody that defines the medina in my mind.

Leashed monkeys are trained to take money (and occasionally cameras) from tourists, while red-suited water vendors in their bright red hats hung with multicolored dingle balls, costumes unchanged in centuries, offer brass cups of water, a tradition left from ancient caravan days. Jugglers and fire breathers supply diversions for the pickpockets whose nimble fingers daily relieve distracted tourists of their wallets. Gallabiyahs (long traditional robe) and kufiyahs (flowing checkered cloth held in place by a black forehead band) outnumber baseball hats and sunglasses here. As I sip my chocolate coffee, I notice a woman with henna-dyed hands looking my way through the slit of her burka, her stylish high-heeled shoes clicking on the ancient ground while she sips a fruit smoothie through a straw under her veil. For the men, especially the elderly, beards long and flowing as their robes are the order of the day.

By mid-morning it is a nonstop, no-rules sea of humanity, where anything can be had if you know the right person, and a few extra dirham might bring forth a hidden treasure from under a vendor's table. If you don't have a connection, money takes their place. It is the romance of the Kasbah meets Barnum & Bailey; where Alice's rabbit hole has come to life and people watching in Marrakesh makes Times Square seem lifeless.

So, it was from my corner table each morning that I would nurse my coffee and jot notes for future stories. Ideas fell as hail in a storm as the endless parade of costumes, smells, and even personalities could easily overload the senses. In the afternoons I would take a wide, meandering stroll through the maze of vendor's stalls, passing street musicians with their swinging hat tassels twirling in time to their playing and marveling at the endless colors and embroidery patterns that gave life to normally drab burkas. I followed my nose to burlap sacks full of saffron and turmeric offered by toothless old women smoking hand-rolled cigarettes and avoided eye contact with the young boys decked out in hennaed eyes that suggested unthinkable acts.

One could not help but be bowled over by the sheer spectrum of items offered. Endless rows of tables held watches that told no time, bowls of animal teeth, pirated CDs, decades old cigarette packs, knockoff designer jewelry, and endless knick-knacks culled from endangered species. If you can dream it, you can buy it in the medina, and so, it was in this cornucopia of the bizarre that I spotted the train.

It was an ingenious little toy. A white turbaned Osama Bin Laden sat on a skateboard on a circular red-and-blue plastic track no larger than a hand towel. Behind him, George W. Bush, clad in military fatigues and sitting astride a double barreled gun, pursued him in an armored vehicle straight out of a Mad Max movie. Both figures were about an inch tall. George's "tank" held a single AA battery that drives the tank, and a magnet on each vehicle repels the other as Bush chases Bin Laden in a never-ending circle; the epitome of tourist kitsch imitating life. It was so tackily cool, so current, so…MARAKESH! As soon as I saw it I knew I had to have it.

Now that was a couple of years post 9/11, and much of the world was still leery of travel. By my reckoning, there were not that many Westerners in the medina at that time and our presence did not go unnoticed. While on the road, I try to maintain a low profile, but I am continually told that I "look American," whatever that means, and being large with a California accent usually gives me away. Perhaps that day it was my Leonard Cohen T-shirt and wrap-around shades that gave me up, but eyes turned my way when I walked by. Still, I was blindsided by how quickly my wonderful discovery segued into a bad B movie.

My first reaction at seeing the train was one of those nervous, split-second laughs that come from deep inside of their own volition to embarrass us at inappropriate moments; like giggling when you slice a finger open. It was more of a startled exclamation, and yet it was enough to stop the conversation of four vendors who were sharing a morning's cup of tea from a communal samovar and whose eyes turned as one in the direction of my verbal faux pas, fixing me with a stare of utter contempt; a stare so vicious it carried the physical weight of a slap. They were hard men, men of the desert, used to settling disputes at the point of a knife and whose faces carried scars that spoke to that fact. I was on unsteady ground.

I picked up one of the pre-packaged trains and held it up with a polite smile to suggest that I wanted to buy it. The smallest of the four men, his head wrapped in a dirty kufiyah, with that perpetual look of always needing a shave, stepped forward to snatch the package from my hands while spitting out an Arabic invective along with his saliva. He was livid, glaring so intensely I could taste the hatred. His message was clear; no infidel was going to buy his plastic Bin Laden.

With a polite nod I turned to walk away but the little man came after me, waving his arms and announcing my evil deed to all within earshot. My momentary lapse of cultural sensitivity began to snowball.

Now, I have always tried to consider both sides of every issue, especially while on the road, and was quite aware that I was in a Berber, Muslim country, while my own homeland was actively fighting other Muslims, but, in my experience, most people make a distinction between benign travelers and their war-mongering governments. The bottom line was that I had done nothing intentionally wrong. I was simply a Westerner and the toy train raised a touchy subject at that time and place. Still, I should have tread more lightly.

The little man continued to follow me, yelling and gesturing like an Italian traffic cop, and he was beginning to attract a crowd. I picked up my pace, hoping to lose him in the general crush of people. I passed several other toy trains for sale but did not stop for any of them. It was time to get out of Dodge.

By now, there were five or six curious onlookers joining the posse and the little agitator who was now on a roll, had them whipped into an anti-tourist, no-plastic-train-buying mob. They looked like giant chess pieces ready to do battle, lined up in their robes and turbans, some fingering curved daggers in their sashes, talking as much with their hands as their voices. It was a gathering of testosterone looking for trouble.

I turned a corner to lose myself in the maze of the souk but paused only a brief second to look behind me, and at the sight of the robed posse I broke into a cold sweat. I was now prey, being hunted on the enemies' home ground. I could make out the word "American," being floated about and it did not sound flattering. I had to flee.

The adrenalin was pumping as I beat a hasty retreat, doubling back in alleys and ducking into small shops to see if the lynch mob was still on my trail. For a while, it seemed that I had lost them.

I turned into a hole-in-the-wall bakery with heart racing and added the caffeine of another cup of coffee to think things through. After years of travel in remote places, even those where I might have expected hostility, it was the first time I had been confronted by it based solely on my nationality and it was unnerving.

My mind was sorting through all of this when I looked up to see a small man in a checkered kufiyah staring at me through the café window freezing me in a moment of fear. I did not recognize this fellow from the medina. He wore glasses and his robe was finely embroidered which set him apart from the rest of my trackers. He was obviously zeroed in on me, or was I just paranoid? Wondering if I had been cornered by the mob, I rose to find the back door when the little man broke into a lop-sided smile and raised his palm for me to sit. He walked into the bakery, shuffling his slippered feet like a young child who had been caught stealing, and pulled one of the packaged trains out from under his robe, placing it on the table in front of me behind a shy grin.

When I managed to close my mouth, I fumbled for some bills to pay him but he held up his hands to say no. We had no common language but there really was no need. I could see the embarrassment in his eyes. His simple act was an apology for his countrymen's actions.

I don't think he could have followed me, so apparently he had simply wandered through the souk until he found me because he thought it the right thing to do. That realization caused guilt, fear, and bewilderment all to collide within me—guilt for my cultural insensitivity, fear of the crowd still following me, and bewilderment at hostility being suddenly replaced by simple kindness. This jumble of feelings was mixed with gratitude for the finest expression of humanity my travels have ever gifted me.

I offered him a chair and he asked the waiter for juice while I ordered a third coffee. For a moment we sat in silence, eyes locked in understanding, our unspoken words needing no translation. I can still remember his tobacco-stained smile that trailed off south toward his jaw that said more than any words could.

Since that day I have often reflected on that afternoon and the little man who brought me the train. I think of him every time I look at it on the shelf in my garage. Every so often I set it up on my dining room table and watch the endless pursuit go round and round.

In April of 2011, a militant cell claiming a connection to Al Qaeda blew up the Argana Café in the medina killing 17 and wounding 25. The same people that passed my table at the café and entered my notebook to give me this story were likely the same people that fell victim on that terrible day, and as I sat there writing I was unaware that at the time the silent forces that launched the Arab Spring were already in motion, ready to sweep across north Africa and the Middle East in a cultural tsunami.

Now when I prepare for a journey, my friends ask how I can travel when it is so dangerous, and I always tell them that travel is necessary if we are ever to have a lasting peace. Only by continuing to meet new people in new places can we ever reach mutual understanding. Only by traveling can we attain the realization of how much more difficult it is to strike someone you know personally than it is to hate someone you know only from electronic sound bites.

Anyone who passed by our table that day and saw an American in a Leonard Cohen T-shirt sharing a drink with an Arab Muslim in a kufiyah would not know that it was a simple child's toy that brought us together. They would not know that two thousand years of suspicion and mistrust were melting away over coffee and a juice drink.

What they would know is that one of us had to travel to get there, and because of that, we had found common ground.

Moussa and his rifle

To Live or Die in the Danakil

THE SIX GUNMEN ARRIVED AT SUNSET, BOUGHT AND PAID FOR, and all we had to do was choose who would go with whom. Moussa was quite small as Afar tribesmen go and yet, everything about his manner suggested he was a predator. He squatted in the sand, chin to his knees, his opal eyes darting back and forth, missing nothing. Slowly producing a bone-handled blade, he began to sharpen it on a stone next to him, gently, methodically, running it back and forth, and as I watched his movements with interest, I remember wondering as I chose him whether he would protect me or kill me.

I had received the call only two weeks prior from our friend, a volcanologist for NASA at the Jet Propulsion Laboratory in Pasadena. She was leading a group of planetary scientists to study a rare shield volcano in the northern Ethiopian desert and wanted me to write about the journey. My wife, Irene, never one to be left behind, signed on immediately. We were going to the Danakil Depression, home of the Afar people. I also naively assumed that with all the doctorates on board for this journey, NASA would be monitoring our every move by hovering satellite, ready to pluck us from the jaws of danger. I was wrong.

The Afar are Sunni Muslims and hereditary nomads who number about 1,500,000 spread throughout Eritrea, Ethiopia, Somalia, and Djibouti. Their history can be traced back at least to the 13th century when they first appear in the writings of the noted Moroccan historian Ibn Sa'id. They are sometimes referred to as the Danakil as they are closely associated with the great desert of the same name.

They were introduced to the general public in *Arabian Sands*, an epic travel book by Wilfred Thesiger, who crossed their land in 1935, calling them murderous thugs among other non-mentionable titles. By the mid-20th century, there were numerous reports of them castrating trespassers on their land. This frightening reputation aside, they were also known for their exceptionally kind treatment of animals, especially their camels that they consider to be family members. The African Ass, extinct throughout the rest of the continent, thrives in their desert due to their protection, and while they might dis-embowel a trespasser, they would never intentionally step on a plant or flower.

Their homeland, in the Danakil Depression, is arguably the hottest and most barren wilderness on Earth where temperatures hover around 120 degrees, (48.8 Celsius) and they pay homage to local caliphs while recognizing no other government. Our destination, the Erta Ale volcano, vents its wrath in the center of that land of endless salt flats and brown blowing sand. It is sacred to the Afar in ways not easily understood by outsiders.

The Afar stayed pretty much off the international grid until 1998 when Eritrea and Ethiopia fought a stalemated war on their land, and since that time they have had almost complete autonomy as a buffer between the two uneasy nations due to their violent nature. They are single-handedly credited with keeping Al Qaeda from crossing the Red Sea from Yemen into this part of Africa. All of that aside, the Danakil has experienced numerous kidnappings for ransom over the past few decades, the credits for which have been claimed by just as many splinter terrorist groups.

Only a handful of Afar have assimilated into city life while even fewer make their living by cutting salt blocks from the desert floor under a relentless sun that they sell to the camel caravans. Each block brings them a rough equivalent of one U.S. dollar. Only recently have the clans that live near the Erta Ale volcano begun to admit trekkers, realizing this natural inferno to be a cash cow tourist draw. Their reputation and social skills aside, as it is in many cultures with no written language, their word is their bond, even unto death, and it was their word that saved my life.

Only after we arrived did we learn that NASA had refused funding and logistical support, labeling the journey "too dangerous," and so we were on our own. At that point I considered backing out, but logic came in third after curiosity and adventure. The Afar offered us access to the volcano provided we each hire one of them to act as security. So what could go wrong?

This is a situation most explorers have to confront at one time or another, to trust a man with a gun who says he will protect you for a price. It is a roll of the dice and the bet is one's life. Who knows why we do such things? It seems an inbred human flaw that our curiosity often results in our demise and yet many of us return to possible danger like moths to a flame. Such questions butt up against the meaning of life itself, a pursuit so far that seems to elude mortal man. I have no death wish, but I prefer to meet it doing what I love rather than lying in a hospital bed one day wondering why I never chased the dream. And so we went to Ethiopia.

From the capital of Addis Ababa we flew northeast
to the city of Mekele, still reeling from Eritrean artillery
with cratered streets and shop windows covered by hastily
nailed plywood boards. Tuk-tuks plied the streets carrying women wrapped in long shawls with hennaed eyes to
shops riddled with bullet holes and shell hits whose shelves
mostly sat empty of goods. Those we passed walking had
the thousand-yard stare of combat veterans. In a surreal
encounter, I chanced upon a desert tortoise wandering
down the main road, his shell heavily dented, probably
due to a shrapnel hit. The tortoise seemed an appropriate
metaphor for the city itself, slowly moving forward, damaged but recovering.

From Mekele, an eight-hour drive by Land Rover took
us past countless artillery craters, burned-out armored
vehicles, and towering sand dunes that dwarfed us like
rogue waves, deep into the Danakil. There is nothing like
vast desert to make one realize personal insignificance.
Our two small vehicles raised such a cloud of dust as to
announce our presence long before our arrival.

In the late afternoon, we pulled into the Afar outpost
of Dodom, a rambling shanty town of homemade huts
populated by sarong-wearing young men with Kalashnikov rifles slung lazily across their shoulders. A handful
of women, wrapped in long shawls, watched us with hennaed eyes, warily from the shadows. All we needed to do a
scene from *Arabian Nights* was a film crew. Money changed
hands, loyalty oaths were sworn, and we were escorted to
stone huts to await our night ascent of the volcano. It was
supposed to be a three-hour trek to the summit.

It was too hot to sleep or eat and I could not force
down hot water without retching, so my personal stage
was set early for disaster to come. Our intrepid group lay
in a row inside the hut, panting like lizards and willing the
temperature to fall, knowing it would not.

Irene had one good eye and the trail, such as it is, being razor-sharp basaltic andesite lava, made us decide that she would ride a camel while the rest of us would go on foot. Our escorts arrived at sunset, and that is when I chose Moussa.

Feral as he was, he oozed an undefinable quality that shown through his eyes and moved my gut to pick him. His black hair was a mass of curly ringlets that stuck out like a weed bursting through concrete in search of sunlight and his skin carried the hue of dark chocolate. He had that African look of a protein-starved diet but his arms and legs were taught as bowstrings. His conglomerate costume of rags approached nakedness and where he got the purple crocs for his feet is anybody's guess. And yet, something told me if I was going to be in a gunfight, I'd want Moussa next to me.

Irene mounted her camel and was led off by her gunman as the rest of us fell into a single file to negotiate the uneven terrain under a moonless night. Our headlamps, bouncing off volcanic boulders, cast dancing shadows all about like a macabre puppet show, accentuating the eerie ambiance of the evening. It was viciously hot and the earth trembled as we walked up the volcano's flank, a mere 600 feet in altitude gain over six miles to reach the churning cauldron of the lake at the summit. The deep indigo sky slowly revealed pinpricks of light as the Milky Way began to arch over us like a hazy silver rainbow.

The Afar, in their ragtag attire, cast off from previous trekkers, walked noiselessly over boot-lacerating ground in their plastic sandals and rubber flip-flops. Their bodies carry no fat. They are burnt and dried by the sun until they resemble walking mummies, drained of all moisture; some faces etched by tribal scarring. Their rifles were extensions of their arms, rarely set down and never out of their reach. Every noise and each peripheral movement brought a reaction that only those who live in a war zone can give. Some had grenades hung from their belts that if exploded near the hardened magma would intensify the shrapnel a hundred fold. All of them had a dagger tucked in their belt. Up close, most are a mass of scars and more than a few have a milky eye from blowing sand. They are warriors from another era; first and foremost, warriors for whom tempered steel is how differences are settled, and they are always at war with someone or something.

The Afar moved like wraiths and within minutes our group was spread over a vast area of the slope, hidden from each other by massive boulders. Irene was out of my sight and I was questioning the importance of our being there. In the velvety blankness, Moussa would disappear for minutes at a time and then my headlamp would pick him up, squatting on top of a boulder, eyeing me like a cat ready to pounce.

My breath came harder with each step, which I chalked up to advancing age and three plus decades of remote exploration, but after two more hours I could go no further and collapsed, sucking air in great gasps. I assumed it was a heart attack and remember looking up at the stars as the earth rumbled beneath me thinking it was such a beautiful place to die. I don't remember how long I laid there and I may have passed out until I focused on the barrel of an automatic rifle aimed between my eyes. Moussa was straddling me, poking me with his Kalashnikov. From my haze, I vaguely recall saying a prayer for Irene and waiting for Moussa to pull the trigger.

At that moment, he laid down on the ground next to me, rifle under his head, wrapped himself in his robe, and within a minute he was snoring louder than the mountain. The absurdity of the situation hit me and I burst out laughing.

I was dying on the side of a convulsing volcano in a remote desert, next to a sleeping nomadic gunman, while my wife rode off into the night on a camel. You can't make stuff like that up! It would be one of my greatest stories and no one would ever know it happened! It would die with me! I laughed until I was gasping for air and that awakened Moussa. Standing over us was the camel he had brought down from the summit; Irene's camel, and only then did it hit me that she was safe at the top and that Moussa had come looking for me when I did not show up. My murderous gunman had come to my rescue.

He helped me to my feet, holding me upright, both hands on my shoulders, and held my gaze in his own for several seconds, asking without words if I was okay to continue. I felt no pain but my breath was drawing hard and there was no place to go but up. I looked ahead and saw the red glow of the summit, like a dancing aurora, no more than 100 yards away. I waved off the camel as it would have taken more effort to mount than to walk the final route. If it killed me it would be an appropriate death.

Together, arm in arm, we walked drunkenly toward the crest, and for a second I imagined us as Hillary and Tenzing summiting Everest together, not that our journey was even a fraction so epic, and in hindsight I realize the absurdity of such a comparison, but that was my state of mind at the time.

We stood at the volcano's edge for only a few seconds, gazing into the churning stew of liquid earth belching up from far below. Gas bubbles exploded like fireworks showering burning, liquid confetti in all directions. Under better circumstances, it would have been the light show of a lifetime. Irene found me in the dark and I staggered into her arms as Moussa directed both of us into a grass hut and I drifted off to sleep wondering why anyone would have built a grass hut at the edge of a live volcano.

It seemed only minutes later that Moussa was prodding me again with his rifle and I heard our party yelling to pack up fast. Dawn was just beginning to break when a gunshot ended the night. I was still in a blank haze and not thinking rationally at all when Moussa waved us down the trail and Irene led me off on foot. Within a hundred yards two more shots rang out. This time we heard the zing as the bullets passed overhead and we dove for cover.

When you are being shot at you do not think. It might take a second for the whine of the bullet to register for what it is, but once it does, life becomes extremely intense and you merge with the ground, becoming a part of it. In this instance, the ground was flesh-lacerating magma.

Moussa was yelling and frantically waving us downward while aiming his rifle uphill when Irene stood up and fell over. At first I thought she had been hit, but her foot had lodged in a rock crevice and it twisted her ankle so severely she could not stand. In an instant, Moussa was there with the camel and together we pushed her on top with no saddle, smacked it hard on the butt, and sent her careening down the trail away from the gunfire.

I descended fast as I could with Moussa at my side, my breath coming in short gasps. Every few seconds he would whirl backwards, his rifle leveled to fire, but there was no more shooting, and after a while he seemed to relax. I had no way of asking him what had happened and doubt that he would have told me if he could. Perhaps the Afar were simply letting off steam, or having fun at our expense, or just maybe, one or two hotheads decided that killing us was preferable to guiding us as the money would be the same.

The next few hours are a hazy memory that seems like a dream recalled. I mechanically put one foot in front of the other and it took no effort to keep my mind blank. There was no sense of movement over the vast desolation, it was just too immense. My breaths still came with difficulty, like when someone has punched you in the stomach, but I was alive and in no pain so I just could not allow myself to consider any more than that. Each step was one closer to Irene.

Hours and many miles later, I collapsed again in a hut back at Dodom. My electrolytes were depleted and my body was involuntarily cramping into a fetal position. Irene, sure that I was dying, forced dry Gatorade down my throat that revived me enough to stand and helped me to the Rover. In my haze, I was looking for Moussa to thank him and to offer him more money when the other Afar started yelling and I heard magazines being slammed into rifle breaches. I was pushed into the Rover and we took off with tires spinning, sending a rooster tail of sand into the air. No one shot at us as we drove away.

I never found out who had fired the shots at the summit or why, and I never saw Moussa again. My malevolent gunmen proved to be a guardian angel who has haunted my dreams ever since. Many times I have awakened at night, gasping for air while staring into a rifle barrel. If ever a debt was left unpaid, it is mine to this man, and all I can do now is pay it forward in the future.

Returning home we found that Irene had a fractured fibula and spent a month in a walking boot. I had multiple blood clots in both legs and lungs that accounted for my faux heart attack. Three different doctors told me I should have died on the volcano. It took me one year to recover. The scientists got their data, and I got a great story.

A few months later, nine trekkers were awakened from a sound sleep inside the same grass huts on the summit of Erta Ale. According to the BBC, they were manhandled outside where five of them; German, Hungarian, and Austrian, were lined up and executed with AK47 Kalashnikov automatic rifles. The other four disappeared into the desert night.

Responsibility was claimed by the Afar Revolutionary Democratic Front Militia, the same tribal faction that Moussa was from.

The author with his ancestors

Conversations
with a Caveman

MDU SQUATTED ON A LARGE BLOOD-STAINED ROCK, HIS CHIN resting on his knees as he prodded the cooking fire with a small tree branch. His eyes held mine as he stoked the embers, studying me as he had done all day on the hunt. He was somewhat feral but with that same gleam in the eye that betrays deep intelligence.

His kinsmen stood behind me as the bloody baboon meat crackled and sizzled directly on the open flame. They waited respectfully for me to take the first bite, offered by their leader, as my mind raced with endless mistakes I might commit as a guest in such a situation. Ancient societies live by ceremony and I was learning those of the Hadzabe in real time as I went.

I looked around at those wiry men the color of wet mud with their baggy shorts held up with braided roots and took in the highway system of veins that stood out on their whippet thin arms and legs. They are men who pull bows that can drop an elephant and shoot birds on the wing; they hit their target on the run and can run all day. I was now sitting among them, about to eat seared baboon that two hours prior might have killed me.

When I first arrived, Mdu was standing on an outcropping of granite boulders in front of a cave entrance from which issued the sweet smell of a wet wood fire. The cold granite glistened from its fine coating of rain and the mud tried to suck off my boots. His head was encircled with a halo of baboon hair that I assumed was his mantle of power as none of the others wore such decoration. He pounded his chest twice with a fist and spread his arms wide, as if to say, "This is my land," implying the vast panorama of the Manyara highlands that enveloped us in western Tanzania. His enormous bow, slung across his thin shoulders was taller than he was and I could not help noticing various animal skins spread over rocks to dry in the sun. He was an impressive sight with the Great Rift Wall behind him.

I lowered my head, acknowledging his dominance and with that he beckoned me inside the entrance where his diminutive kinsmen eyed me warily, and where my attention went immediately to the enormous bush knives they were using to slice meat on the open fire. Simply allowing me to approach was a personal coup but I would also be tested. Mdu stamped out the small fire with a leathery foot and walked me through the ceremony of making a new one with two sticks, kindling, and some steel. To record this momentous occasion for prosperity I set my mini-tripod on a rock, set the camera timer, and ran back to make fire. Their looks of incomprehension at my actions made me feel quite stupid, but I admit to never hesitating to make a fool of myself to record a good story.

After three failed attempts, a tiny puff of flame sprang to life and apparently it was sufficient, because after that, I was handed a carved bone pipe stuffed with local weed. Mdu lit it for me with a burning twig he took from the fire with a bare hand. I took a short draw before handing it back to him. It was potent and went straight to my head. I did not want to be stoned in this situation, but it was necessary if I was to enter their society. They all laughed as I hacked and coughed.

Having no common reference points, I reminded myself that I was among people attuned to the rhythm of the earth. They lived by the cycles of nature. For them, there was no division between the spiritual and material worlds and suddenly, there I was, a creature from a different planet. They did not smoke weed to get high but to reach an altered state of consciousness beyond my current comprehension, a state I was unused to entering myself. I had to cast aside all preconceived ideas, think on my feet, and react to them in the moment if I was to penetrate their society; all of that while being jacked on local ganja.

The Hadzabe are true Bushmen who, like their Saan cousins from Namibia who became unwitting film stars in *The Gods Must Be Crazy*, speak the Khoisan click language. They are not just nomadic, but only build temporary shelters for the most dire of weather conditions, preferring to sleep on the ground or in caves, and when they make a significant kill, the entire village will relocate to feast upon it. They use iron tools thanks to their willingness to trade meat with the local Barbaig people who are master blacksmiths, but the Hadzabe themselves have never reached that level of sophisticated toolmaking. They wear beaded jewelry that they have traded for with the Maasai, warriors who surround them in this valley, outnumbering them by 300 to one. While most of the estimated 3,000 existing Hadzabe have assimilated into cities to live on government subsidies, this isolated pocket of hunter/ gatherers, estimated to number less than 300, is barely removed from the Stone Age, and they have no desire to join the present world.

So while early man and I sat staring at each other I felt a physical presence creeping upon me like a ground fog. Perhaps it was the collective consciousness of mankind that permeated the land since Mdus's forefathers sat where he was, or maybe it was just too much history and emotion for this traveler to absorb. Sitting around a fire with a clan of cave men was not just extremely cool, but physically intimidating and emotionally exhausting. I had removed my watch and ring before arriving to prevent them from becoming talismans or being appropriated as unwilling gifts, but Mdu was still fascinated by the buttons and zippers of my clothing. He ran his fingers over both like a blind person seeing through touch. He ran his hands over my arms and through my hair while turning to comment to his clansmen as though delivering a medical lecture about a specimen. He pointed at objects around the fire, naming them in clicks and seemed amused when I repeated his words as though I were a quick learning pet. The others seemed to have little or no interest in me; I was simply there and had no bearing on their lives. However without my knowledge, I was about play a much larger role.

Suddenly, Mdu stood up so I did too. He grabbed his bow and arrows and we exited the cave, trotting down a muddy trail into thick bush. Mdu would stop and squat, pointing out minute scratches in the soil or bent leaves that I assumed were signs of an animals passing, and he watched me intently to make sure I was taking it all in. Sometimes he froze in mid-stride and sniffed the air, and at any little sound his bow was instantly knocked with an arrow.

He melted into the surroundings, silently, as much a part of the forest as the trees or animals and he pointed at things in branches I could not see until I realized that he was talking to me like a teacher to a small child. Why else would I have approached him if not to learn? I was happy to be his student.

He would squat there in the dirt staring at me, unmoving as I tried to enter his mind. I lost track of time and miles as I walked by his side, conscious of passing through time before recorded history. Hundreds of generations of Hadzabe had walked that trail, but I may very well have been the first white man. Language was not necessary as the moment was pure emotion and experience as Mdu passed on to me a sense of complete merging with not only the spiritual, but with the natural environment as well. In his presence I reached a mental state I have rarely achieved on my own. As we continued in silence, I wondered if I really was what men like him would become in a thousand years' time.

He clicked away as we walked, seemingly oblivious to what I may or not have understood. I pointed out a contrail in the overhead sky and wondered if it meant anything to him other than a bird or spirit. At that point, he gave a great sigh as though I was just not getting it and began a lengthy bout of clicks mixed with words that I found fascinating. He was gesturing all about him and was quite the orator, making me think that he was giving me a grand lesson on the universe but I was just not smart enough to take it all in. He finished with a foot stomp to emphasize all that he had said was final. With that he turned and walked away. It was quite a tirade and I thought perhaps I had just heard the Big Bang Theory from someone whose oral histories began with it.

He would disappear into thick brush then pop back out and beckon me to follow. I always found him crouched, observing a small creature that was unaware of his presence and unworthy of his arrow. One of those times I lost him for several minutes and he did not reappear. It was then that I thought I heard him coming through the undergrowth and was surprised at how much noise he was suddenly making. I froze in place just as a large and very enraged baboon broke cover no more than 20 feet from me. It was shrieking and stomping its foot, its hands balled into tight fists. It should be noted here that baboons are fierce predators who will not hesitate to attack a man. They are the main diet of the Hadzabe and react accordingly when approached.

The next few seconds are related as if in a dream because I froze in the moment and only recall flashes of memory. Before I could move, I heard the dull thud as the points of two arrows pierced the animal's neck. Suddenly, the baboon, who moments before was poised to rip me to shreds, lay before me twitching from the neurotoxin on the arrows that was ending its life. Both were clean kill shots. Mdu stood to my right while his man was on my left; both already had arrows knocked in their bows. I had not heard either one of them nor was I aware that they were that close.

Mdu's man had trailed us without me realizing it and Mdu had used me as bait to draw the baboon out. They had me covered the entire time and had demonstrated a perfect example of a coordinated hunt. The realization that he had used me like a tool was slowly being tattooed on my memory. With adrenalin pulsing, I had no time to be angry at what might have cost me my life. At the same time, the writer in me was already thinking, "What a story! Who will believe this? "I WAS THE BAIT!"

I watched in stunned silence as Mdu pulled his knife and severed the animal's head, then gutted its innards with deft strokes, while his wingman shouldered the dead beast like a backpack and took off down the trail. Mdu approached and streaked my cheeks with the creature's blood; acknowledging my part in the hunt, then he knelt to spread the dirt until no sign of the kill was left in evidence. He handed me his bow to carry on the long walk back to the cave and I considered that an honor. That night the baboon skull would hang in a tree with the bow suspended from it in order to take the animal's power for the next hunt.

I felt tears through the drying blood on my cheeks as emotion took over; not only from a wild animal attack, but also my dramatic rescue, and my acceptance by this hunter/gatherer clan. My day was an avalanche of emotion, from expectation to anxiety, to comradery, fear, and pure joy, and after we climbed the small rise back to the cave entrance, I slumped to the ground in a heap, spent in body and spirit. I reached for a notebook to record my thoughts but found my hands shaking too much to write. How do you describe something you are certain no one else has experienced?

Sleep took me briefly but I awoke to the smell of burning meat, and I was brought back to the moment by Mdu kneeling to hand me a sizzling piece of seared baboon, but first he leaned in to touch his forehead to mine. At that moment I felt connected to all of human existence.

Since that day I have thought of Mdu often. I imagine him sitting under a silver moon, stoking a fire, smoking his ganja, telling tales of days on the hunt. His life seemed quite simple compared to mine but then we all have our baggage and I am sure that even a bushman, unencumbered by material goods, has his own demons. I have thought long and hard about what my life would be like had I been born an African Bushmen because the circumstances of our birth, something that none of us can control, is all that really separates any of us. I believe I would be happy.

It was only after my return home that I came upon a long-term DNA study of the Hadzabe conducted by Stanford University. In 2003 their research paper declared that they are one of three distinct primary genetic groups from which all of mankind has descended. If that is correct, I had met my own ancestors...as the bait...on a baboon hunt.

Has this story affected my life? Oh yes.

More than once, I have awakened in a cold sweat a second before an angry baboon sinks its fangs into my throat, and one time I exited a dream while rubbing imaginary blood from my face. Other times I simply relive sitting by a fire eating seared meat with cave men in animal skins and I smile. The romantic in me has imagined the dinner conversations that would have gone, "Did you hear? He was torn apart by a wild animal in Africa!" For good or bad, such an experience is never far from recollection. Travel by definition gifts us with unique moments; moments that become memories, memories that turn into stories, and stories in Africa become both legend and history.

The Hadzabe gave me this story. I hope one of theirs is about the white guy that unwittingly helped them kill a baboon. If I am a story told around their campfire, then I have served an even higher purpose.

PART FOUR

Emotional
Journeys

Downtown Moscow

A Kiss for the Condemned

IRENE AND I WERE FINISHING A QUIET DINNER IN THE PICTURE window of a restaurant on Tverskaya Street, the main drag of Moscow, when the salt and pepper shakers began marching across the table.

We Californians looked at each other and simultaneously said, "Earthquake!" A low rumble escalated rapidly like a movie soundtrack of an oncoming dinosaur that segued into the crunch and clank of moving steel. We ran outside to join a rapidly gathering crowd just as a squat, green line of Russian armor crested the horizon.

A squadron of T-90 battle tanks filled the street, two abreast, coming on like a slow-motion migration of mastodons; the yawing ovals of their cannons loomed like hungry mouths. The ground trembled and buildings shuddered; the people stood by silently. Was this a coup? For us children of the Cold War, it was terrifying.

The tanks were followed closely by a rolling mechanized juggernaut, including truly massive ICBMs mounted on trailers, and the thought did occur that one of them might be targeted at my own home. It appeared that the entire Russian army was pouring into downtown Moscow.

Outside, on the street, hordes of mute Muscovites, frozen in time like Pompeian statues, bore silent witness. There was no sign of emotion from the people, no sounds; they occupied neat rows silently awaiting their fate. That was our welcome to Russia.

We found out later that this overpowering diorama of steel and aggression was a rehearsal for the gargantuan military parade through Red Square on May 9th, the single most important day in Russia. On that date in 1945, Germany surrendered to the Russian army in Berlin, ending the war in Europe, but not in the hearts and minds of the Russian people. Seven decades later, that day is imbedded in their DNA. The rape of the motherland by Hitler's armies has been imprinted on the souls of the survivors, and passed down through generations like a hereditary disease. Veterans and the elderly favor the term "Great Patriotic War," and impose their stories onto visitor's lives.

We left Moscow on a small riverboat traveling up that brown artery of Mother Russia's lifeblood, the Volga, looking for locals with tales to tell; the logger drinking a beer with a raw herring for lunch, the businessman who looks over his shoulder before speaking, and the babushka who lost five sons in the battle of Stalingrad. Those were the Russians we wanted to meet. Those of us who spent our childhood waiting for the "Russkies" to drop the big one on us wanted to look the bogeyman in the eye even if he has grown old and gray like us now.

For several days on both sides of May 9th, life in the Volga villages reverts to 1945. It is supposed to be a time of celebration and a respite from daily life that for many has not changed in generations. It is a time to remember the glory days when outnumbered defenders turned back invading hordes. It is a time for stories to be exaggerated and for old men to be young once more. It is a few precious hours of fantasy away from big brother, and nowhere is this week anticipated more than in the onion-domed villages that hug the Volga.

Veterans walk the streets in moth-eaten uniforms that no longer close over their bellies, faded rows of medals upon their chests, limping from wounds never truly healed, while babushkas wear the shawls and aprons they hauled potatoes in during the hard years. Everyone, young and old, sports the blue-and-orange Ribbon of Saint George, an anachronistic reminder of days when Imperial Russia had hutzpah, and men strained their vodka through great flowing moustaches over stories of cavalry charges into machine guns. All of rural Russia reminisces at ceremonies that welcome visitors like us, so corpulent mayors can take pride in reminding the world of how much they have suffered. Twenty five million dead in the "Great Patriotic War" is their common mantra.

In villages such as Uglich and Yaroslavl—both former battlefields—the permanent memorials, carved in stone, were overwhelmed by avalanches of floral bouquets. Some of them hosted small eternal flames. At midday, in the town squares, crowds gathered to recite poetry about dead heroes while rows of old ladies, widows of long dead soldiers, received flowers from pretty teenaged girls in vintage war uniforms. Several hamlets seemed to have the same central icon, a crumbling concrete anti-tank barrier known as a dragon's tooth; some held many, dotting the fields like asphalt mushrooms. There, ancient men knelt with tears streaming to touch the names of former comrades scratched into the stone. Shell and bullet holes in homes have been left unrepaired as reminders. In rural Russia, the Second World War remains a living breathing entity.

Officially, the week is a celebration of their victory, a victory whose price tag was way too high, and is in fact still being paid by the despair of its people, but celebration is a misleading word for it. In Moscow and Saint

Petersburg, it is a public secret that real power rests in the hands of those who thumb their noses at the law. Women in furs ride in flashy cars driven by men in thousand dollar suits, but such affluence does not trickle down to the masses that occupy the countryside, and nowhere is that more apparent than along the river.

As boat passengers photograph the towering bronze of Mother Russia, rising like the Phoenix from the center of the Volga and pointing the way to Saint Petersburg, few of them are aware of the 200,000 graves beneath their keel, all of them slave laborers Joseph Stalin worked to death to build the canal they are sailing on. The seagulls pooping on the statues head are a proper metaphor.

Uglich is a speck of a village that has squatted on a dog-leg of the Volga since 1148, but locals claim its birth was 937 A.D. Not much has changed in the interim. So, it seems appropriate that the first sight river travelers have of Uglich is the bloody red church with the cerulean onion domes that stands on the site where the youngest son of Ivan the Terrible had his throat slit by an assassin. That is Uglichs's claim to fame; at least it was until we arrived.

No sooner had my wife and I stepped ashore to accept bread and salt as a traditional greeting from a girl in peasant dress than she inquired if we might be Americans. She told us of an elderly lady in town that had yet to meet one of our kind and was extending a dinner invitation to her home that we immediately accepted.

The gravel path took us through a town where time halted two centuries ago. It was a shuttered and decrepit collection of rotting wooden buildings leaning at angles like a deserted movie set, surrounded by a spindly forest of alders under a dark gray sky. A feral dog barked at our arrival and that halted two scarved and shawled grandmothers in their tracks: Looking as though they had seen the Gollum, they retreated into a nearby home.

Just past the tiny river port, on a hilltop covered with a blanket of sheep, we found the Stalinesque concrete block-houses that represent Soviet architecture to the Western mind, looking more like bunkers than housing; row after row of dull gray apartments, their only individuality being their unit number. Other than a tiny brown and wilted tomato plant in the process of giving up the struggle, no life was in evidence. Bleak was the merriest adjective I could assign to the neighborhood.

Just then a yellowing lace curtain parted in a tiny window that could just as easily serve as a gun port, and perhaps did, when the German Wehrmacht occupied the town. Through the curtain, the outline of a feminine face appeared for a second, then, from a dark hallway, backlit by a single yellow bulb, our hostess emerged, slowly, tentatively, like a sloth waking from sleep. She was diminutive, dressed in thrift store chic that has defined rural Russian fashion since the days of Karl Marx.

After a few silent moments of mutual staring, she burst forth in that nervous giggle talk that raises our voices an octave when confronted by the uncomfortable and unknown. Our lack of a common language did not prohibit her from unleashing a nonstop torrent of Russian as she encircled both of us in a bear hug while chattering like a chipmunk. Apparently, she was a woman who required no other person to conduct a conversation.

We stuck out our hands and said our names. She jerked a thumb her own way and said "Tatiana," holding the second A with enough emphasis for it to sound like a purr. Inside her tiny home, we found a neat and orderly lair filled with personal mementos and the ubiquitous photos of men in uniform staring solemnly at the camera.

A small black-and-white television sporting rabbit ears with tin foil tips occupied the center of a bookcase full of novel-sized covers, validating my belief that Russians love their great authors. It was the kind of place where men play chess, women gossip for entertainment, and home socializing is restricted to weekly meetings of the socialist workers party.

In the kitchen we passed a man with the face of an apple doll and hands of an outdoor laborer, sitting quietly at the table, staring into a coffee cup as though it was filled with information. His only acknowledgement of us was a slight nod of the head. Our hostess gestured toward him in an offhand manner as we passed through, making us think of him as possibly her husband, but at the moment, of no real consequence. In a dining room the size of a walk-in closet, a table was set for several visitors with aged china, ringed in gold, of various sizes and designs, the kind that gets passed down through generations. The simple grandeur of the place settings was overpowered by the glass and plastic chandelier that hung over it all. Tatiana was hoping for an array of visitors, but we were it.

Without slowing her machine-gun monologue, she produced a decanter of local vodka, the sort that will ignite from a match at twenty feet, and showed us how to interlock arms as we drank our shots while staring intently into each other's eyes. Russians drink vodka like fish swim, learning to do so at about the same time they begin to walk. For a non-Russian to keep pace is impossible, but Tatiana urged us to try. We took seats while she disappeared into the kitchen, never hearing a sound from the fellow sitting there alone. She returned with one bowl of food at a time, following each one by an arm-linked downing of booze. The final table setting was a modest offering of boiled potatoes, coarse dark bread, and hand pickled gherkins, whose home jar she proudly thrust under my nose till it watered.

After four shots of her homemade brew, Irene and I were more than ready to float some food in our liquid filled stomachs when Tatiana stood for what we both hoped would be the final toast to international goodwill and world peace. I downed my shot as we gazed into each others' bloodshot eyes. In one quick motion, she slammed her glass down on the table, turned to grasp my face with both hands in a claw like grip, and planted a full on, open-mouthed tongue probe square on target that took me completely by surprise. She held on like a remora sucking on a shark with a kiss that would have made Gustave Klimt proud. In my surprise, all I really recall was that she tasted of cigarettes and pickles as her fingernails dug into my cheeks. I am also sure it was the only time since our introduction that she had ceased talking. When she released me, she demurely flattened her apron with both hands and sat down as though nothing had happened, passing us the potatoes and re-commencing her running commentary, proving my theory that she needed no one but herself to hold a conversation.

Her assault was so quick and smoothly executed, so unexpected, that Irene and I could only exchange glances and continue with dinner. We ate modestly and hurriedly, politely refusing more drinks, hoping to exit without further unanticipated traditions taking place. Tatiana chattered on, pecking at her food and grabbing my arm for emphasis after each proclamation, but without any more eye contact.

We stayed long enough to think it polite, and then bid our farewells without a common word being exchanged. Tatiana walked us to   door, hanging on my arm like a drowning woman grasping a raft. There, we received a farewell hug and I braced for a second lunge that never came.

Irene and I walked down the path in knowing silence. What had happened was not a kiss; it was not even slightly sexual. It was a primal scream. It was the desperate act of a condemned woman frantically grasping at an impossible fantasy, if only for a second. To her, I was America, that vast unknowable land of awe and wonder where everyone is rich and wishes all come true, and for that moment, she held her wish in front of her to taste it for perhaps her one and only time. I was America, a land that only came to people like her through black and white sound bites on a tiny screen, but enough for those like her to build a dream around. For that moment, Tatiana shed her life of hardship and escaped into that dream as only one used to depravation could understand, and in that moment, she became a butterfly.

I hope she took something of value from the encounter if only a flash of memory to comfort her on dark Russian nights, but I think for her it was a story she will tell her friends and grandchildren over and often, the story of how an American grabbed and kissed her, and it will grow in size and passion with each telling because that is what a good fantasy should do. For me, it remains one of those unforgettable kisses like a first date because few of us are ever present to witness the baring of a human soul.

Irene took my hand as we walked down the path to the boat and I stopped just once to look back. I thought I saw a face watching us through the yellow lace curtains.

A Stone for Henry Leman

WHEN I FIRST MET HIM, HENRY LEMAN WAS ELDERLY. HE had the melancholy air of one who had been broken, and yet carried himself with an old world dignity. His wife, Berte, had recently died, but he still got up each morning and went through the rituals because he knew no other way.

His daily uniform was a starched white shirt with rolled sleeves over pleated black trousers. His penny loafers were always immaculate when he wore them but mostly he liked to pad about in white socks.

I had delivered his mail for several months when he appeared at the door one day and invited me in for coffee, and as he spooned massive amounts of sugar into his cup I saw the tattoo. I knew what the six tiny numbers on the inside of his left forearm meant, but he saw me looking and quietly whispered, "Auschwitz." Henry was a survivor of the most infamous of the Nazi death camps.

Postmen rank equally with bartenders and priests in that everyone who knows them wants to talk. They are, in fact, the only active profession that physically goes to a person's home each day to provide a service, thus making

Auschwitz, Poland

them ready-made listeners for all who wish to bear their soul. Henry's eyes told me he needed to talk.

He told me most of his friends were gone and he seemed a bit lost in the cavernous silence of his home. He had no children because his wife had been sterilized in the camp at Dachau years before, but somehow the two survivors found each other in the aftermath of war. They had a pact not to discuss what either had gone through, but when Berte died, the ghosts came searching for Henry, and Henry came to me.

I've had many theories about why he chose me of all people. He had no idea that I was also a writer who sought such tales, and had he known, perhaps he never would have related them. I guess Henry just had a feeling about me. To me, it was the start of a sad, but great adventure.

So, with that first cup of coffee, we began a series of dialogues that lasted until his death several months later. I took no notes; it was much too personal for that. His details were such that I rarely had any questions to ask. We always sat at the dining room table and he always served strong black coffee in Daulton china cups with gold trim, the final remnants of a bygone era. Henry made me late on my route countless times, but our visits were worth it.

He would sip his coffee and relate to me the most gruesome tales of torture and survival, all said as a matter of fact with no discernable hatred or bitterness attached. From the start, I felt he was still trying to make sense of his past and at the same time, insure that his story did not die with him. He was testifying the only way he could.

He was a twenty-year-old student when the Gestapo came in the night, his last ever in Vienna. He recalled passing out from the human stench after four days without food, water, or bathrooms, but was unable to fall because so many people were packed together like produce inside the boxcar that ferried them to Birkenau, Poland. They were greeted there by the "Angel of Death" himself, Doctor Mengele, who immediately chose victims for his sadistic experiments while deciding life or death for everyone else with a flip of his glove to one side or the other. To the immediate right were gas chambers; to the left, the work camp of Auschwitz, only a kilometer away. There, Henry's name became a tattoo number and he was put to work with the Sondercommando, dragging bodies from the gas chambers to the crematorium.

Although I knew what happened in those camps, hearing the stories from one who had survived brought them to life in a most gruesome manner. Sometimes I had trouble listening, even though Henry appeared almost like a small boy relating a bad dream. Some of his tales were simply beyond my comprehension, as I had never personally witnessed that underbelly of the human race. He usually ended his stories as he finished his second cup of sugar-laden coffee and I would go home then, unable to sleep. I filed his stories away, deep inside, knowing I would have to write about them one day but wondering if, or when, I would have the ability or courage to do them justice.

A decade later I felt it was time.

My wife and I were on a train in Eastern Europe, knowing we would end up in Auschwitz, but putting it off until the end. I immediately recognized the main gate from historic photos. The curving wrought iron sign overhead said, "Work will set you free" in German. As I stepped across that most infamous of portals, I felt Henry standing next to me. He wore blue-and-white striped pajamas with a pillbox hat. There was a yellow star sewn haphazardly over the left breast and his tattoo number, 976843 was stenciled over the pocket. He was young again; stick thin, with eyes deeply sunk from terror.

I looked left and right down the double row of barbed wire fences at multiple guard towers that once held dogs and machine guns. Aging and faded wooden signs warned inmates to halt ten feet from the wire or be shot. Henry told me the fences had been electrified and that many prisoners, unable to take the abuse any longer, would fling themselves onto the fence to end the misery. With that, he touched the fence to send sparks flying, but I know I am the only one who saw that. The electricity was cut in 1945.

He walked by my side as we entered the first barracks where a hundred victims had been crammed onto a cold stone floor in a room designed to hold maybe twenty. Inside the doorway was a large quote from George Santayana that read, "Those who do not learn from history are doomed to repeat it." His hand on my lower back urged me along. We passed entire rooms filled with human hair, children's shoes, people's luggage, prosthetic limbs, and all the countless accessories of normal daily life that had been stripped from the inmates along with their dignity. The other barracks were the same, glass-walled dioramas filled floor to ceiling with tiny pieces of lives cut short. I was unable to take my eyes off the room full of little girls' dolls, all staring vacantly, waiting for their playmates who never returned. By the time we left the compound the collective sorrow of Europe hung like a thick fog.

Each building held its own tale of horror and suffering that reached a crescendo in the SS holding cells. Henry led me down the dark stairway lit by a single naked bulb. There, in tiny dark cubicles, below ground with no windows, narrow enough to touch all walls while standing in the center, unspeakable tortures were applied to those who had no information to give up. People who were guilty of nothing other than being a Jew or Gypsy, or in many cases, simply being educated, spent their final hours in these cells, crying with pain, trembling with fear. I could barely make out the word "mercy" on one wall in dried blood. The only exit from those cells was the path to the gallows or gas chamber. It was there that I first saw the ghosts.

When you walk through Auschwitz you see ghosts. I saw hundreds. There is nothing supernatural about it, there are no holograms or trick mirrors: Their spirits are wedded to the place. You can hear them whispering their stories as they pass you. They hold your gaze because they want you to listen and to know. In just four years of existence, Auschwitz tore a giant hole in the collective consciousness of mankind and left behind the shattered essence of too many souls for them not to be seen. Incomprehension of man's cruelty washed over me and trampled any vestigial belief I had in inherent kindness. Because of that place, humanity could not be completely whole again.

Next, I followed Henry to the "Killing Wall," a simple stone slab where those no longer useful as human guinea pigs or too weak to be worked to death, were summarily shot. He pointed low on the wall to the holes where the bullets passed cleanly through the young children. Next to the wall were the hanging poles where those condemned to live a bit longer were left to dangle, their feet off the ground, their hands tied behind their backs, as they were jerked upwards by ropes around their wrists until their shoulders dislocated. Henry bent over to show me how he had been hung.

I sat for a moment, debating whether or not to leave at that point, empathy for those interred under our feet, bearing down like a physical weight, but Henry stood in front of me shaking his head that we were not through yet.

The gas chambers sat low and squat, concrete bunkers with sod roofs, neatly framed by a beautiful forest only a few yards away. We stopped at the massive steel door to peer through the tiny glass porthole where SS guards watched countless thousands asphyxiate inside as Cyklon B, developed as an insecticide, spread its deadly fumes into innocent lungs. Sometimes people gasped for up to a half hour. This is where Henry had worked, handling bodies. I hesitated at the door and he pushed me through, intimating that he could go no further, but that I had to.

Two and a half million lives were ended in that room for the simple fact that they were not Aryan. With a nod from Henry, I fell into line with the ghosts filing in one by one. I stood in the middle of hundreds of the dead and with closed eyes imagined the gas pellets being dropped through the ceiling vent. I heard them drop and begin to hiss like vipers as they released their deadly vapor. I felt myself choking and sucking for air and I was silently screaming like those all around me, but then I opened my eyes and I was alone in deafening silence. A dull bulb illuminated the room, its floor streaked black from the bodily fluids that exit a body upon death that no amount of cleaning can eliminate.

I forced myself into the next room with the giant ovens whose fires consumed the mortal remains. Even though the ovens were scrubbed clean decades ago and the walls disinfected, there is a pervasive stench that reaches the visitor's soul. The smell of burnt flesh is something never forgotten. My stomach was tied in knots, my hands trembled, and my eyes were filled with tears as I stepped outside into the brilliant sunshine of a beautiful day, realizing I was gasping. Henry was waiting for me. He was crying too.

Together, we walked behind the crematorium to a rotting wooden gallows where the camp commandant, SS Obersturmbannfuhrer Rudolph Hoss had been hung in 1947 for crimes against humanity, but I felt nothing. No price was sufficient to balance the debt he owed. It was Hoss who introduced Cyklon B as an efficient killing tool, allowing the SS to murder 2,000 people per hour when the ovens were operating at full capacity. It was his own written estimates that claimed close to 2.5 million people died in his gas chambers, while another half million died of overwork, starvation, beatings, or simply gave up the will to survive. Ironically, the Nazis were among the world's best record keepers and documented every atrocity, often with photos. It was that Teutonic efficiency that finally sent many of them to the gallows after the Nuremberg trials. When Russian soldiers entered the camp on January 27, 1945, Henry was unaware that the last of his guards had fled the previous night. There were 7,500 people still alive in the camp. Henry weighed 92 pounds.

He whispered in my ear that this story, told so many times before, still needed to be repeated, not just now but every now and then, lest the prophecy of Santayana come true. With that, he told me he was going to be with his Berte and he left me for the last time, merging with the other ghosts.

Two decades had passed since I sat down to that first coffee with Henry Leman. I came to believe he picked me as a confidant because I was convenient and for no other reason, but I am grateful that he did. He was a constant reminder of the kind of person I wanted to be. He was at my side as we walked through that camp and his ghost still enters my thoughts often. I am sure he knows that his story is being told and I know he is now happy with his Berte.

As we walked toward the gate to exit I remembered an old Jewish tradition of placing a stone on a grave. This was not Henry's grave, but it came pretty close. I approached the barbed wire and took a final look back. The ghosts were disappearing inside the compound. I picked up a stone from inside the gate and carried it just outside the camp where I left it.

Henry Leman was finally free.

The Watts Towers

Homecoming

As a child in Los Angeles, if I stood on my tiptoes on the roof of my parent's garage, I could see the tallest spires of the Watts Towers. That roof was my youthful sanctuary where my imagination turned the towers into far away mountains or castle turrets that I would explore one day. The towers were whatever I wished them to be, my portal to exotic places found only in magazines, and on the rare occasion that my family would walk to see them, they were too magical to be real, like an apparition.

At the tender age of four, my white, Scottish-German parents bundled me into their '52 Buick for a cross-country odyssey to California to escape both their family and the Illinois winters. My sole recollection of that journey is of my trying to grab a rattlesnake somewhere in the never-ending expanse of Texas, and my father jerking me violently away.

That was 1953 and California issued a strong siren call to the greatest generation still recovering from a war. Hipsters wore zoot suits, and low riders cruised Whittier Boulevard four inches off the ground. The Lawrence Welk orchestra played on a barge off the coast of Santa Monica, and I watched my parents dance to his music on local live television. It was the dull and quiet

Eisenhower era and we quickly found out the only place we could afford to live in sunny Los Angeles was a suburb called Watts.

Watts was the West Coast Harlem then, considered a ghetto by some. It did not matter to my parents that we were the only white people in sight. Within weeks they had found work and I was being cared for by a black lady after school until my folks could pick me up at night. I did not think in terms of black and white then. A color-blind neighborhood accepted us as their own, and I was probably six before I had a white playmate.

A quiet truce existed between white and black in Los Angeles at that time. It was an accepted but not publicly acknowledged, separate but equal apartheid, that I, in my Midwestern shell, was totally oblivious to. So that August in 1965, when the police rousted a black motorist for a traffic violation, the pent-up subterranean anger of half a city boiled over into a week of looting, arson, beatings, and total civil unrest. What came to be known as the Watts Riots was my universe imploding.

We had recently moved to a more mixed-race suburb but the only world I really knew, the black world, was on fire. We sat mesmerized by the television, watching our adopted home self-destruct. My family hunkered down for a week, confused refugees behind enemy lines. For several nights, I slept sporadically between gunshots. When I returned to school I found myself looking over my shoulder. I did not understand the anger of the black community nor the white response to it. It was the first time that life hit me between the eyes.

Trauma has a way of burrowing into one's psyche. We fool ourselves by assuming that since the event has passed, so has the damage. That is rarely true. I was about to go out into the vast world on my own for the first time, and because of that

life altering week, I found myself thinking the same preju-
diced thoughts as the rest of mainstream white America.

I left home soon afterwards and years and careers came
and went as a travel writer's life slowly embraced me.
That life carried me around the planet until somewhere
between Timbuktu and Ouagadougou, the words of Mark
Twain began to make a lot of sense; "Travel is fatal to prejudice, bigotry, and narrow-mindedness, and many of our
people need it sorely on these accounts." It was certainly
what I needed.

Just as Mister Twain said it would, my wanderings
revealed the equality of all mankind and helped put to
rest the dark images of so long ago. I had dropped a lot
of baggage in my travels and felt the need to return to
where I started. I went back to Watts after five decades,
unsure of what I was looking for, and afraid of what I
might find.

The neighborhood was a time capsule of the Eisenhower years, dull and unchanging, just the way its denizens
wanted it to stay. Spanish stucco bungalows hid behind
wrought iron bars and gated lawns and most walls were
frescoed with what would only much later come to be
known as graffiti. It still held the veneer of a rough and
tumble barrio, but the undertone of menace was gone.
The war zone I recalled had patched its wounds and now
bore its scars like a champion fighter. I followed my old
neighborhood's train tracks north to the towers.

Five decades changes ones perspective and seeing them
again triggered not just memories, but emotions. They
were not nearly as tall as my child's mind remembered
them, but their power over me had not dissipated.

They are not a grand opus of artistic creativity like
Gaudi's Sagrada Familia in Barcelona whose general shape
they mimic: they are, in fact, the opposite, simple and plain,

like the gypsy souled immigrant who created them as an act of love to the city that took him in.

They are the creation of Mr. Simon Rodia, a tile mason by trade, but one gifted with the ability to raise craft to high art. Rodia was born in Italy in 1879 and came to America in 1894 where he wandered from place to place until finally settling in Watts in 1920. The following year he began building a series of towers on his land, baffling his neighbors who thought him mentally unbalanced. They could not grasp that his was a labor of love and a thank you to the city that had given him a better life

But to understand what this man has done, you must get up close and personal, because the Watts Towers are at once a monumental work of both architecture and art, and as you look even closer, they are the finest possible metaphor for a city composed almost entirely of people from other places. Rodia spent years collecting the cast-off detritus of the poorest section of a vast metropolis. His silhouette was a common site in the early morning haze that coats the Los Angeles basin a quarter of the year. Wandering the railroad tracks where the transients and poor dumped their refuse, he would return home each afternoon, arms full of discarded chunks of others' lives, and work through the night imbedding all of it in his creation. Broken coffee cups, pieces of glass, shards of tile, dolls heads and more all found new life in the growing monument. Neighborhood children brought him bits and pieces of green glass from their soda bottles, immortalizing the drinks of the times; Squirt, 7 Up, and Bubble Up. Wonderful deep blue glass came from old milk of magnesia bottles.

The concept was simple, seventeen interconnected towers made of rebar, wrapped in wire mesh, and coated with concrete. Rodia lived in a small shack among his towers and his miner's headlamp was a familiar light to the neighbors as he spent the darkness imbedding his found shards into the concrete.

It is difficult to consider the towers without also offering a simple comparison to the work of his fellow Italian, Michelangelo Buonaratti; between the tile cutter and the stone cutter. Two obsessive geniuses who worked day and night, forsaking any sort of normal life, devoting years to superhuman tasks of creation, one to a city, the other to God. No, the towers are not the monumental achievement of the Sistine but they are a symbol of hope for the working man, a title both artists were proud to own. Michelangelo labored at his task for three years; Rodia for nearly three decades.

Rodia tried many times to explain that his towers were a metaphor for Los Angeles, representing all the disparate cultures, religions, and languages that made it a city from somewhere else. He referred to them as "Nuestra Familia," our family, but the times were quite ignorant. The towers were frequently vandalized during the rare times that he left them. The city labeled them an eyesore and tried to have them demolished, saying they would be unsafe during an earthquake, but when engineers tried to pull them down, they held fast, refusing even to bend. As Rodia aged, his health declined from a life of hard labor and he tired of battling bureaucratic red tape. In 1955, he "quit claimed" his towers to a neighbor and moved to Martinez, California, where he died ten years later at his sister's home. After his departure, the tiny shack he had lived in mysteriously burned down. There is no mention of him ever returning to Watts again.

Ownership of the towers changed hands numerous times and eventually they ended up on four separate historical registers, while they are currently under consideration to be named a UNESCO World Heritage site. Rodia died without knowing his towers had become the symbol

of the city. In recent years the towers have appeared in
dozens of movies, countless television shows, been mentioned in Broadway plays and been referenced in literature
and song. Today, they are an international landmark.

Seeing them after five decades was not just a homecoming, but a minor epiphany, as I understood for the
first time what Rodia was trying to accomplish. In them
I still saw the faraway places of my youth, but now they
were tempered by the imagery of my own travels in the
real world. The towers were not just a microcosm of Watts,
or even Los Angeles, they were a vision of a world come
together, and for me personally, they are a manifestation of
everywhere I had been, but had I not journeyed so long
and so far, I most likely would never have realized that.

I sat for most of an afternoon staring at the towers
and letting them take me back to so many places. I sat
there for so long that an elderly lady approached to ask if
I was alright. I assured her I was and we found ourselves
engaged in a most pleasant conversation. Her home was
directly across the street from the towers and she had lived
in Watts her entire life.

When I told her of my family's move there so long ago
and of the black family that had cared for me as a child,
she seemed startled. She asked my name but did not know
me, and when she asked for the name of the lady who had
cared for me, I could not recall.

She stared at me for several seconds then gently took
my hand in hers. "When I was a youngster, my aunt cared
for a young white boy in the afternoons. He was the only
one around so everybody knew him. If that was you, then
you and I might have played together as children."

We walked to her aunt's old home, but time and mile-
age had dulled my memory so I could not say if it is where
I spent so many afternoons, but that did not matter. I chose

to believe that it was her aunt that had taken me in and that she and I had been childhood playmates.

My life had taken me around the world and deposited me back where I had started. While I sat there thinking about all of that, some words from the great travel correspondent, Martha Gellhorn came to me, "As a traveler I have learned that it is wise not to return to what was once perfection."

I did not go back to find perfection. All I needed was a homecoming.

Our "maids"

Limping Home
from Kashgar

IT WAS OUR LAST NIGHT IN KASHGAR, CHINA, AND PIERRE and I lay on our beds waiting for the phone to ring.

The calls had come like clockwork, every night at 11:00 sharp. The sultry female voice would ask if there was anything we needed for the night, and every night we would politely decline and then giggle like schoolboys with a secret.

The old Soviet Embassy building had maintained a bordello for its mostly male staff, and our room, now part of a "foreigner" hotel, was pale pink and green with lavender accents, lace doilies, and plastic flowered sconces. At least there was no mirror on the ceiling, but the nightly phone call told us some of the current staff still plied their former trade. Though free to come and go during the day, the compound gates were locked nightly at nine, effectively making us prisoners. The double click on our phone line whenever we would hang up was a steady reminder that we were traveling in a police state.

My musings on China have always alternated between love and hate; love for the ancient myths, ceremony, and humanity of its people: hatred for the tyrannical regime that has ruled it with an iron fist my entire lifetime. It is unfortunate, for the Chinese people, that countries with vast populations are usually governed through fear and intimidation. This seems the only means of controlling numbers that could overwhelm their overseers should they ever become organized or literate. It is this fear of information and knowledge that arrives with every tourist from a free thinking country that terrifies the powers that be, making every visitor suspect.

I declared myself a retired school teacher on my entry visa for two reasons; Teachers command great respect in China, and journalists of any kind must pay a heavy "tax" on their cameras. Even so, I have always drawn bureaucratic attention with the three cameras I carry to document my stories, and long ago I accepted inflated "foreigner" prices as being the norm for Westerners.

It had been fun watching the Olympics on local television but frustrating that we could only see Chinese athletes. Each time foreign athletes were about to perform, the Communist-party-controlled television network would switch to nationalistic commercials or display the red flag and play martial music in their place. So my final night in China was passed locked inside a pink bordello, listening to military marches, and sipping warm Singha beer with a 70-year-old man in his underwear.

In the morning, the old mamasan—that we had been calling "the hen"—had all the girls lined up in their starched uniforms to bow us on a safe journey. We assumed that she was the former madam and her girls, mostly ethnic Uyghurs, and thus second-class citizens, were given a choice after the Russians pulled out; return to mother Russia, or work as hotel maids in China; maids with benefits as our nightly caller implied. I bowed to the hen, but before I could grab my bag she pulled me into her tiny

curio shop just off the lobby in a final attempt to relieve
me of my last few yuan.

I had already politely passed on all of her tourist trinkets but this time there was a strikingly beautiful walking
stick lying on the counter. It was aged bamboo that time
and personal use had given a wonderful golden patina that
when struck by sunlight, shaded into a smoky brown. The
grip was a hardwood I could not identify and had been
gloriously worked into a mythical dragon's head, the kind
often employed as a temple guardian. It spoke Mandarin
to me, pleading for a home. I had been ambushed and
we both knew it. The hen had found my weak spot. The
bartering was quick and bloody. I had to make my flight
so I paid her price, grabbed my prize and headed for the
cab to show Pierre. He thought it was a dandy and since
both of us collected walking sticks, we discussed them all
the way to the airport.

My bag was so jammed that I had duct taped the zipper to insure it did not burst in transit, so I decided the
simplest way to get my cane home would be to use it as it
was intended. At the airport curb, I shuffled up and down
in a Chaplinesque kind of rolling walk, leaning on it awk-
wardly as I had never used a cane before. Pierre made fun
of me, saying I kept switching the leg I was limping on. We
were both just having fun.

Within a couple of minutes an official-looking gentleman in a suit was at my side with a wheelchair, bowing
me to sit down while he shouldered my bag onto the back
rack and whisked me inside leaving Pierre standing there
with his mouth agape. In the spirit of the moment, I just
waved to Pierre and laughed it off. We were ushered right
through security with barely a passing of a wand. Once
past the metal detectors, a second gentleman came zoom-
ing up in a golf cart, lifted my bag on board and turned on

a flashing yellow light and loud beeping siren that made the crowd part as if we were an ambulance.

I never expected this kind of treatment and was enjoying myself immensely although starting to feel a bit guilty about having left Pierre behind. My thoughts were cut short when the golf cart driver accelerated through the enormous duty free shop, zipping past hundreds of faceless passengers trudging to their respective flights, all craning their necks to see this obvious VIP being motorcaded through the airport. At the check-in counter a second wheelchair was already waiting and two burly attendants made sure my transfer went without incident.

At this point, I was deposited next to the boarding ramp amongst a line of elderly people in airport wheelchairs, all in need of pre-boarding assistance. It looked like God's waiting room. They put me first in line, next to a lady so old she resembled an apple doll, who pulled down her surgical mask to reveal a wide smile full of betel nut-stained teeth. She reached over and patted my hand then said something I could not understand but she pantomimed walking with a cane. Now I really began to feel guilty. This is not what I had intended at all. I did not want to mimic people who were truly challenged in some way, I just wanted to get my cane home, but the act had gone too far and there was no turning back now.

An announcement came over the PA and an attendant started to push me toward the boarding entrance but I protested, pointing at the others and telling him to take them first. He leaned over and quietly whispered in my ear, "Please sir, you are a foreigner and must go first." I realized then that he was being watched and no doubt would be severely reprimanded if I did not go first. This was the China I knew so well, the China concerned first and foremost with the façade they presented to the outside world.

They had not brought a wheelchair to me because I was limping, but because I was a "Westerner" who was limping.

This was the class-conscious China that used the army to round up the homeless of Beijing and move them to the countryside during the Olympics so the world could not see them, and it was the China that does not allow citizenship to its minorities. It is a country that wishes to play on the world stage, but treats its citizens as though they are less than nothing.

Self-guilt or not, at this point I was all in. They wheeled me to the airplane door where I stood up, and leaning heavily on the cane, made my way into coach while being hovered over by a concerned flight attendant. No sooner had I sat down than she offered me a drink and I gratefully accepted, knowing a Chinese passenger in coach would not have received the same offer.

In a few minutes, the general crush of passengers began to file on board, pushing, shoving, and throwing elbows as is the local custom in a Chinese crowd. Pierre was swept onboard in the human tide until he fell into the seat next to me, laughing and punching me hard on the arm to punish me for abandoning him.

Before we took off, the attendant appeared with a beautiful young Chinese girl at her side. She asked if I would mind switching seats with the young lady who had been sitting in business class and wanted to give up her seat to the foreign gentleman with the cane. I knew that she had not volunteered to do this.

Before I could say anything, Pierre answered for me with an even stronger punch to my arm. He was not going to miss this opportunity, so I rose and bowed to the young lady, who took her seat next to Pierre who was already waving for me to leave, and so I limped forward into business class.

It so happened that my new seatmate was an antique dealer who immediately commented on my cane, and after a few pointed questions, offered me a sum almost three times what I had paid for it. Since this entire story revolved around the cane, it could not be told properly if I sold it, so I politely refused the offer.

China cannot help being itself with its ingrained class-conscious caste system. There seems to be something in the national psyche that each generation passes on to the next: a belief that one group of people is better than another, in general this being the Han majority. Perhaps it is national guilt for this feeling that makes them worry so much about what foreigners think of them. Each time I return to China I cannot wait to get there, but each time I leave her I am saddened to see such a grand and ancient lady self-immolated by so many prejudices.

As the plane climbed out of the smoggy haze of Beijing, I watched the shape of the city merge into dark gray silhouettes, making all landmarks undefinable. It seemed a most appropriate exit from a country that is itself, a giant paradox.

Death and Remembrance

IN THE SUN-TOASTED DESERT OF SOUTHERN BAJA, MEXICO, there is a lagoon where divergent species have come together for centuries. It is the halfway point of an annual 14,000-mile migration of the Pacific gray whale.

It is a place of sanctuary where they are not hunted. They come because they know they are safe there. It is, in fact, a giant nursery where young calves learn to survive, because gray whales are born with limited natural instinct and must be taught the fine art of being a whale.

This lagoon is the only place on earth where wild animals, in their natural habitat, routinely seek human contact, and where for 18 seasons I have worked among them as a guide and naturalist. It is a place of magic where dreams are fulfilled and fantasies come true.

When I need solace and introspection it is where the sounds of nature drown out those of man, where the vast horizon is ringed with purple mountains and rolling sand dunes, and where coyotes sing you to sleep with towering arias to the moon. It is a land so vast and wide open as to reduce the mightiest ego to a grain of sand; part of the

The orphaned whale

Vizcaino Biosphere, where a quarter of the Baja peninsula and all of its creatures, are under federal protection.

Mother whales approach our boats with their calves to show off their handiwork, and our acceptance of each other as equals is immediate and lasting. They are benign giants who desire our companionship, and I have come to know individuals who return here year after year.

But the ocean is a harsh master and there is a natural death rate among these creatures that is heartbreaking. This story is about one of those deaths...and how it revived a life

Much of my free time in San Ignacio is spent in a kayak, gliding silently through miles of shallow channels lined with mangroves. There I lose myself as just one more cosmic speck in the universe. Countless sea birds that line the shore have no fear at my approach, and rainbow colored fish huddle beneath my hull, while red and orange crabs scurry along the bottom, running from overhead shadows. Osprey soar high overhead before diving like kamikazes to take surface fish and the seagulls have learned to drop clams on the rocks to break them open. To all of them, I am an errant log floating by, a simple observer of the grand ballet of nature that performs each day on this epic stage. It is a land rich with life, but tempered by the equality of death, and it was on such a morning that I spotted the dead whale.

We call them floaters and they are a natural byproduct of a 7,000-mile swim that brings these creatures from the frigid northern waters of the Bering and Chukchi seas north of Alaska where they summer. Part of my job is cataloguing such heartbreak, and I approach this whale to look for an obvious cause of death.

She is a mature female, perhaps 30 feet long; her side stove in, most likely from a massive wave cutter that is so common on the prow of today's cargo ships. As she rolls back and forth on the tide, voracious gulls have already begun to strip the carcass. By tomorrow the crabs will find her, and in three days, all that remains will be a skeleton. When it comes to death, nature is an efficient mistress. I know this whale by a large white saddle patch on her right flank. I have seen her before. As I circle her I am stunned to find a calf huddled close, nudging her, trying to awaken her. This mother had no calf when I encountered her two seasons ago. Grays bear their young every other year after a thirteen-month gestation. I figure this calf to be no more than a couple months old, and without its mother, the end will come soon.

Grays are not known to adopt orphans, and a whale this young is entirely defenseless, let alone clueless. I slowly back off, feeling myself an intruder, but as I turn to paddle away, the young whale breaks from its mother, and swims to me. She turns parallel, spooning my boat, hugging me as only a creature with no arms can. With her mother gone, she desperately claims me as a surrogate. She presses against my boat and I run my hand along her rubbery skin. This is a phenomenon called transference that is new to me. I am now this whale's universe.

She hangs there in the water, her eye imploring mine, begging for something I cannot give. I am slow to tears, but her grief triggers something deep inside, and suddenly all of my own personal losses wash over me as the animal's pain merges with my own. I stroke the young whale's head; run my hand along the line of her mouth, as tears return me to the day my own mother died.

I could not cry for her then, not real grief tears. Mine was a grief of denial. It took months for the reality to sink in and the depth of that loss to hit me. When it did I was emotionally crippled for a long time, so I buried my feelings along with her ashes, and whenever the memory tries to come back to me, I turn it away.

Now, as I look into that young whale's eye, I am looking into my own mother's, and the past is returning against my will. Once again she is lying on that bed waiting for the end, her smile telling me she loves me and that it is all right, but her eyes plead with me not to let her go. Once more after so many years, that same sense of helplessness blindsides me, and I scream like a berserk demon as the wind carries my lament away, unheard, over the waves.

I want to fight the universe, I want to yell at God, but long ago I accepted the cruelty of life. I know what this whale feels. Now is not my time, it is hers, and now she is my charge and I know what I must do. I slip out of my boat, inflate my vest so I don't have to swim, and hang there in the water with my arms around the grieving whale. It does not fight or move, but allows me to hold it as I cry for both of our losses, hers recent, and mine from so long ago. I am a poor substitute for her loss, but experience has taught me the importance of touch to these creatures. It is all I can offer.

I am unaware of time until eventually I slide back into my boat and head for open water, knowing the newborn whale will follow. If it returns to the sea, death will claim it quickly, and that is preferable to the slow torture of starvation. I paddle hard into the face of the incoming waves and see the little whale trying to keep pace while being overwhelmed by the surf that is reclaiming her.

Bracing against the waves, I pray not to see her again. I yell for God to take her…and then she is gone.

I have been present at countless deaths upon the water over the years but none has affected me this way. How did this animal return my buried emotions to me? I want to believe she is a sign, perhaps even sent by my mother to reconnect with me, but that is just a wishful fantasy.

Alone in a kayak, bobbing like a seabird; all those years of love and kindness come back to me. On the vast canvas of the endless sky, I see my mother's face as I remember her from my childhood, a face that has turned opaque in my mind after so many vacant years. Suddenly she is young and beautiful once more, and her smell envelops me as she takes me in her arms. I too am young again for these fleeting moments, happy as memories return to me, and feeling a peace I have not known since she died. For these precious moments we float there on the water together; the only two people on earth. Locking her inside my heart once again, I turn and paddle for camp as the wind dries all my tears.

We never know what will trigger a memory; the song of a bird, the flight of a butterfly, or even a grieving whale.

Nature is cruel, but she also has a soft side. On this day she took one mother away, but gave another one back.

PART FIVE

Personal Stories

Hermit monk

Photo Ops
with Buddha

THERE ARE PLACES THAT IMBED THEMSELVES INSIDE A TRAVeler so deep that you take a piece of them with you when you leave.

A part of Burma came home with me from a cave high in the mountains.

Pindaya is a fly speck on a map of predominately Buddhist Myanmar/Burma. It sits halfway between Mandalay and Inle Lake on a steep incline that terminates in a vertical granite rock face that can only be reached through a series of steep switchbacks. I had not planned on going there but had overheard a dinner conversation that described an enormous cave system in the mountains that is home to one of the holiest sites in local Theravada Buddhism. Perhaps my newly awakened karma had called me.

Theravada means, "Teaching of the Elders." It is one of three main branches of Buddhism that originated in northern India and Nepal in the sixth century B.C. and rapidly spread throughout Southeast Asia until it was introduced to Cambodia in the 13th century via monks from Sri Lanka. Eventually, it spilled over the vague borders into Myanmar where it dug in deep. It is a personal religion that worships no deity but rather teaches self-control in order to release all attachment to the material world and achieve personal enlightenment. The intensity of its adherents has drawn me back to Southeast Asia many times.

The bus coughs and wheezes as it struggles to climb the steep mountain roads. The driver downshifts often, talking to it, willing it upward, and when we reach the summit, it shudders and dies in a puff of smoke. The driver sits back and lights a cheroot; he is used to this. The road has ended in a large parking lot lined with coffin-sized vendor stalls all hawking cheap tourist trinkets and cold drinks. "Hey Mistah, one dollar!" a man yells as he shoves a plastic Buddha in my face that I politely decline. The vendors are incredibly aggressive toward me which I attribute to my being a rare Westerner and thus wealthy in their eyes.

At the end of the parking lot, a ten-foot warrior is firing his bow at a twenty-foot tall spider. The warrior wears a gold crown to signify his royalty. The spider has crawled down the mountain, from its lair inside the cave. It's eyes bulge and blood drips from its elongated fangs. The statues represent an old Burmese folk tale associated with the cave, but their gaudiness combined with the vendor stalls gives the place an amusement park aura. People are climbing onto the spider to have their photos taken and I am second-guessing my reasons for coming.

At the base of the rock face, I enter a glass-and-steel elevator as out of place with the locale as the spider, and am shot 600 feet into the air where I step out into a different reality. There is a long walkway filled with hundreds of pairs of shoes and nuns in pink and orange robes selling spirit money for the faithful to use as offerings inside the cave. Just beyond this, there is a rush of stale air coming from the enormous yawning entrance to the cave.

Pilgrims are prostrated everywhere in front of towering Buddhas, more than 8,000 statues of all sizes and shapes. Many of the faithful have forsaken the elevator to climb the dizzying stairs on hands and knees. From the entrance on, I must step carefully over and around hundreds of devotees, kneeling in prayer and meditation, slowly moving from one statue to the next in a mendicant assembly line.

The oldest statues date to 1750, and many bear inscriptions from the Konbaung period (1782-1885), the last ruling dynasty of Burma. No other religious site offers such a range of Buddhist iconography or diversity of style and ornamentation. The cave gives physical form to esoteric beliefs, but, like Buddhism itself, it is internal, hidden from the world until you enter its mysteries.

As one raised within a dogmatic faith, I have long been fascinated by Buddhism because to me "religion" has always implied a deity, and Buddhism has none. Yet, the passionate fervor that I have personally come to associate with Buddhists seems based on "right action" a cornerstone of Christian belief. Nowhere is it more evident than in the masses all around me, foreheads pressed to the floor, crawling like inchworms, lost in concentrated faith to the essence these images represent. There are hundreds, if not thousands of people inside the cave, and yet, there is no talking; only the low hum of countless mantras that sounds like an enormous swarm of bees.

The statues are staggered like seats in an arena, disappearing upward into the black vastness of the cave ceiling. The lighting is dim and dramatic, designed to accentuate the immensity of the cavern and to give an aura of mystery to the statues. A meandering maze of paths wanders for miles, leading pilgrims in all directions past one diorama after another. Some trails dead end at ancient meditation cells while one enters a massive cathedral like room where stalactites and stalagmites grope for each other like fingers entwining to pray. There is enough gold leaf inside this cavern to sink a battleship.

The Buddhas seem to turn and follow me as I pass, and in the dim light, they begin to press inward, towering over me. Under the unyielding gaze of hundreds of enlightened ones, I feel a great sense of self-awareness and my own insignificance in the great cosmic puzzle. I can sense such belief in the cavern that should a statue begin to walk, I would not be shocked. The low vibrating OOHMMM, essence of the universe, uttered from thousands of lips, is a palpable presence I can feel in my stomach.

My heart begins to race and I am mildly euphoric. I surrender totally to this feeling, wondering if I am succumbing to the sheer epic of the cavern, or unconsciously tapping into the religious fervor of thousands of faithful; what several spiritual writers have called the collective consciousness of mankind. My walk itself becomes a meditation, a flowing prayer, synched to the cadence of my steps. I have a sense of belonging, of being part of something larger, and a tranquility that has mostly eluded me in the past.

I wander into an area with no people and turn a corner to find myself at a dead end. There, in isolated shadow, I almost stumble over a monk, the first one I have seen. He is a hermit, identified by his cone-shaped leather hat, and probably lives in the cave. He sits silently on his haunches, head bowed, and prayer beads passing through his fingers. His unwashed body odor mingles with the moldiness of the cavern. He is stick thin, an empty rice bowl on the floor in front of him. He prostrates himself before a sitting Buddha, a black hole of a silhouette before a glittering gold statue, each posture mimicking the other in a perfect yin and yang. The image is stunning.

The monk occupies his own reality, oblivious to my presence, and I am too startled to move for several seconds. This tiny space is the only spot in the cave with no other people, and I feel something has drawn me to him in a way words cannot define.

I step behind him, pressed flat to the wall, making myself one more statue while taking in the moment. His low chanting physically captures me and for a few seconds I sense a metaphysical connection to this holy man. My consciousness seems expanded and normal simultaneously, as though I am able to observe events around me from multiple viewpoints at once. The sensation is unnerving as I was not prepared for it and I wonder what power this monk possesses that his mere proximity has caused such a paradox within me.

These are the moments I travel for, moments to which words can never pay proper homage, moments when time stops and experience imprints an image on your soul. I know I should leave but can't make my feet move and I don't want to disturb him. I step over the hem of his robe, trying to back away unnoticed but it is like trying to leave the determined embrace of a loved one. In my rush to flee, I knock over a bowl of money and fruit offerings. The hold is broken.

The sound is muffled by the close proximity of dozens of large Buddhas, but in my mind I have just upset the cosmos and probably thrown the Earth off its axis to boot. I turn to see the monk, still unmoving, hearing none of my irreverent clatter, when a hand touches my shoulder.

It's a young monk, smiling from ear to ear. He helps me pick up the money and fruit as I wait for a cosmic lightning bolt from Nirvana to strike me for my clumsiness, but none comes. He holds up his iPhone and I realize he wants a selfie with me but I must bend in half to reach his level. The young monk races off and returns seconds later with what I assume is his family. Each produces a cell phone and all six of them take up stations around me, each handing off their phone to a stranger to take a photo while I tower over the entire group. I feel like an extended middle finger of an enclosed hand and begin to laugh at the situation. Buddha really does have a sense of humor. This triggers a domino effect. A line of tiny people is gathering, all wanting their picture taken with this sweating Western giant. Only then do I realize what an oddity I am here as cameras flash away and it does not feel right. I have unwittingly become the center of attention and must end this.

I begin to walk, shaking outstretched hands as I go; a celebrity by default. People are pointing at me and I feel far larger than my true size until I reach an upper cavern and gain my anonymity among the crowd once again.

Reaching the exit, I am stopped in my tracks by the stunning view of the valley below. Hundreds of mushroom-like pagodas dot the landscape, their golden or white domes that from so far away resemble Hershey's Kisses. A blue heron flies past a billowing cumulous cloud in an image so stunningly different from the interior of the cave it brings to mind the concept of Maya, in which all the physical world is an illusion. I guess it is harder to leave the monk than I thought.

My mind is racing as I board the down elevator and I am packed hips to shoulders with a dozen Chinese tourists, all of them two feet shorter than I am and all of them craning their necks to look up at me with a wide-eyed stare I have so often encountered in Asia. A single tiny hand rises from the crowd and snaps a photo of me. When the elevator door opens they push each other, pinning me to the wall, in their rush to exit.

Outside, the giant warrior is still shooting an arrow at the giant spider. Several crimson-robed monks, most of them not yet teenagers, strike histrionic poses and hold their upraised hands like claws while they growl and mug for the cameras. My celebrity has been replaced by a giant plastic bug, so my karmic levels must be normalizing.

I walk by the tourist vendors, and the same man shoves a tiny Buddha into my face. This time I buy it as the perfect reminder of both the tackiness and religious fervor of this cave. It is Ying and Yang incarnate.

Climbing onto a new bus I sink into an empty seat and reach into my bag for a bottle of warm water, aware that I have the word "Burma" on my lips.

Kanas shaman

Breaking Bread
in Kanas

IN FAR NORTHWESTERN CHINA, WHERE A SHARK FIN OUTLINE
on a map punches Russia in the belly and divides
Kazakhstan from Mongolia, invisible spirits and deities
prowl the land.

Kanas is one of China's newest national parks, and
bears a striking similarity to Yosemite. For tourists used
to China's giant smog-choked cities, Kanas is refreshingly
green wilderness. It is also an ancient bastion of shaman-
ism, Tengrism, and animism. Of those three, perhaps Tengrism bears explaining as a religion indigenous to central
Asia involving ancestor worship and polytheism, usually
through the use of totems. Mysticism lies upon Kanas like
a blanket and its most famous resident, Genghis Khan,
(Mongol name: Borjigin Temujin) was a self-proclaimed
shaman. Eight centuries after his death, he remains a constant presence.

Many reasons called me to Kanas, one of which was
to witness a total solar eclipse, and that single event presented me with the most defining image of how deeply
enmeshed the people there are with the spirit world. As
the shadow began to pass over the land, I watched men

in business suits and women in heels scream and run into buildings to hide. I watched people cowering inside their cars, and some, caught unawares in the open, simply fell to the ground, whimpering and covering their faces. A few of the ever-present soldiers stood their ground but most pulled their hats over their faces, shaking at their posts. People, that moments before had appeared quite urbane and sophisticated, proved that in that land of mysticism, everyone was subject to its power.

In the rolling, boulder-strewn hillsides, traditional felt yurts of Mongolian nomads, sprout like summer mushrooms. The mountain people begin to ride as soon as they can walk and to watch them in the saddle is to understand how an army of their ancestors conquered the ancient world from the backs of horses. Legend holds that it was from Kanas that the Mongol hordes descended on Eastern Europe. High above, in the treeless valleys, dozens of stone monoliths stand from those days. Many are carved in the shape of men and locals will tell you they were erected during religious ceremonies presided over by the Khan himself as a lasting call to the reining deities to protect his army abroad and his family at home.

Some of the more modern residents occupy the village of Hemu, which masquerades as a town with its rough-hewn log cabins and sod roofs, left behind nearly a century ago by Russian loggers. In housing of either style, a visitor will always find a portrait of and a shrine to, the mighty Khan. They are as common as chopsticks, along with animal bone talismans and sacred fetishes to combat any lurking evil.

The cabin of the ruling lama is identified by an armada of white prayer flags tied to his fence by passing mendicants and a stroll up most hillsides will reveal stone prayer cairns that launch pilgrims' entreaties into the wind. Tuvan throat singers can be heard in Hemu, enchanting the stones or talking to spirits under a full moon, and in the hills, oracles cast bones to read future events. The people of Kanas occupy dual realities, merged into single time, the material and spiritual; the yin and yang of an ancient life in a modern world.

There are few cars about and the ones that are identify their owners as the suited bureaucrats from Beijing that stick out like brown shoes with a tuxedo. They are ubiquitous government watchdogs, terrified that the outside world might learn that China has cultures more ancient than, and equal to, that of the Han rulers. As an outsider, I quickly grew used to their harassment as the price of traveling in a police state. I might also add that those hard-nosed suits from the capital cowered from the eclipse with the best of them.

Now, I am large, even for a Westerner, and the people of Kanas might be called diminutive. My physical size has often drawn small crowds during various travels through Asia, and I was more than prepared for locals that might think me an incarnation of one of the endless cavalcade of local spirits or demons. I am quite used to bug-eyed stares and open mouths that seem to be an integral part of remote Asian cultures when encountering an outsider. While I was quite a local attraction, I can report that I never encountered thrown stones or an exorcism during my stay, but at I am sure that after my soiree through town I had at least made the evening's dinner conversation.

My arrival in Hemu was apparently coordinated by the serendipity that often finds those of us who wander afar. I have always believed that the best experiences come to those who are open to the ambush and so was only mildly surprised when a young boy approached me in town as I was browsing in a pharmacy, examining the sun dried animal parts, potions, and fetishes that are the tools of a shaman.

An elder lady named Mai Pin heard there was an American about, and sent the young lad to find me as my kind are few and far between in her land, and with him, came an invitation for lunch. Never one to turn down a free meal, I followed him like a loyal pet, up a muddy hill, past the reindeer pens that hold those enormous creatures, not for meat or as work animals, but for their antlers that are shorn annually and shipped to Chinese markets where they demand exorbitant prices as aphrodisiacs. At the crest of the hill I turned in time to see my government shadow jump behind a fence post half his girth in size and could not help laughing at the absurdity of the moment. I waved at him and pointed to where I was going.

Outside my hostess's cabin, I found home-sewn bags filled with mare's milk, left to ferment. Large flat bamboo trays filled with square blobs of the thickly curdled milk hung nearby, that when dried by the sun, became a jaw breaking hard staple of the local diet. I heard my hostess calling from inside the cabin, and as I stepped under the bone talisman nailed over the portal, I was relieved to find that I had enough good joss not to be struck down as an evil spirit.

Now, as in town, such a rare visitor demands an audience and I was no exception. Three generations crowded into the tiny room to inspect the strange invader, the baby of which took one look at me and tore into an aria of bellowing. To him I was most assuredly a demon spirit.

Old Mai rose from her seat leaning heavily on an age-rubbed, serpent-headed walking stick that implied her high status, possibly that of a shaman. I was dining with an elder of rank. She held me by my arms and kissed the air above both of my cheeks then lit a bundle of sage, placing it in a cup next to the window. Turning slowly she spread her arms with a slight bow to the four directions and spoke soft words of ceremony that escaped me, perhaps entreating the spirits that were joining our lunch. Mai and her family had the dark, round, moon faces of Mongols, their high arched cheekbones curving like hills under their rising moon black eyes.

Mai Pin wore the pirate-tied headscarf, faded print dress, and knee-high gum boots that are the uniform of a babushka, and, in fact, she was a widow of one of the last Russian loggers to have felled local timber. She was one of many locals to have merged with the Russians who preferred this life to that of their homeland, and, in turn, produced the next hardy generation of mountain dwellers.

Age and toil had bent her nearly in half, her story etched into the lines of a leathery face, but there was merriment in the glint of her eyes. She wore a hand-carved amulet around her neck and her hands twisted like raptor claws under a framework of protruding veins. She was like a large, mobile apple doll, shuffling to an ancient clay stove where she dropped saucer sized gobs of white dough into a pot of boiling oil that momentarily produced golden, fluffy, but completely tasteless donuts that accompanied the sun-baked mares' milk for our lunch. She waved everyone to a long wooden table where seven of us gathered, and everyone motioned for me to sit first. As we did, each person in turn reached out to lightly touch my hand in unspoken acknowledgement that told me I was both welcome and safe.

All of them talked to me in turn and I answered each as best I could. None of us had a common language but that was no deterrent. We had a most wonderful conversation that wandered up one topic and down another using the unspoken vocabulary of world travelers. In fact, looking back now I can say that many of my favorite conversations on the road have taken place with people I could not talk to. Stories went back and forth, and though they might not have understood mine, each face across from me was a study in concentration.

The image of Mai, walking from her stove, wielding a platter piled high with fried donuts generated an image from my childhood that stormed my brain and conquered my attention. Perhaps it was simply her body language, or maybe just my inner need for a familiar connection in such a far-away land, but an old Norman Rockwell painting came to me in that moment. It was a mother bringing the Thanksgiving turkey to table where her anxious family awaited the feast, and suddenly, I was a six-year-old boy again watching my own mother approach. The image lasted only a second and I quickly returned to the present, but it was enough to remind me that those are the moments I travel for.

I have often had such moments on the road. They are the nuanced connections that spiritual anthropologists refer to as the collective consciousness of mankind, and they have gifted me with the realization that the flap of a butterfly wing in Africa can generate a wind in Asia. The miracle is to be present when it happens, and to recognize it. I have done both many times. Those were the thoughts that shot through my brain like bullets while I happily rode a tidal wave of good karma, joss, or whatever the reader may wish to call it, but there are few times in a traveler's life when days are that good.

Mai, her family and I, talked deep into the afternoon. I ate the tasteless donuts and laughed with one and all at stories I could not understand. When the sun began to paint the hillsides purple, I rose to leave and she grasped both of my hands, holding them palms up, and spit into them. She closed her eyes and with her thumbs pressed into my open palms she began a soft guttural chant that the others joined. I accepted it as her blessing, and when she finished, she gave me a smile brighter than a sunrise and wrapped me in a hug that would make any bear proud. As she did this, the others stood in turn to embrace me with a sincerity most people reserve for family. If Mai intuited anything personal of me or where I came from during our visit, then that was her shaman's power. What I took from all of them would fill volumes. They did not care who or what I was, they simply opened their hearts and home to a traveler.

A Cheshire cat smile of a moon rocked low in the evening sky as I walked down the hill toward the village, and in passing, I nodded to my government overseer who was slumped next to a wooden corral, looking quite wilted after spying on me through the long hot day. He would have to make up a story about me in order to make his report to his masters even slightly interesting. Perhaps he could tell them I was one of the wandering spirits of the mountains, a white demon. That at least, would seem credible there.

I laughed at the thought of offering him that idea but he would not have understood me.

Khun-Sa statue, "The Kingpin"

Kingpin

SOMETIMES SPIRITS MUST LINGER WHERE THEIR CORPOREAL bodies spent their time on Earth, unable to leave until coming to terms with past deeds.

In the steaming jungle mountains where Thailand, Burma, and Laos collide on a map, there is a complex of crumbling structures, overgrown with climbing vines and monitored by a praetorian guard of monkeys that loudly denounce visitors. It is not an ancient ruin like so many others in this land but a modern ruin in more ways than one. It is a monument to ruined lives and dreams. It is called Ban Hin Taek, "Village of Broken Stone," and many spirits dwell there.

It is the former operating base of Khun-Sa, a peasant and illiterate thug who rose to become one of the most powerful and wealthiest men of his time. Born to a Shan hill tribe mother and Chinese father in British Burma in 1937, he was the self-proclaimed "King of the Golden Triangle." In his day, he was more powerful then Pablo Escobar, more famous than "El Chapo" Guzman. Heroin was his trade.

An early monsoon ends with my arrival as the steam from a baking sun on wet foliage envelopes the ruin as though it were rising from a cloud. Upwards of 30,000 mercenaries once lived here in the employ of the world's most notorious drug lord who, at the height of his power, was considered untouchable by three separate countries. In this onetime enclave of depravity, gorgeous bromeliads and orchids proliferate while monkeys throw balls of dung at my approach. Stunning red and purple parrots screech warnings from the trees. The ethereal beauty of the place stands at odds with its horrendous past, giving the moment a surreal feeling of it being a movie set.

Khun Sa began life as Chang Chi-Fu, a teenage recruit with the Chinese Nationalist Kuomintang army not long after the Second World War. During the Chinese civil war, the Kuomintang, under Generalissimo Chang Kai-Shek was defeated by Mao's Tse Tung's Communists and retreated to the island of Taiwan while splinter groups fled over the border into northern Thailand and Laos in the Shan state. It was in these mountains that Chang Chi-Fu assembled a rag-tag army of about 600 men and in return for arms and money from the Kuomintang, began to fight a guerilla war against Communists on both sides of the border.

I push open a creaking door and wave aside years of cobwebs to enter a former barracks where heavily graffitied walls speak of the eternal discontent of the common soldier. Here is scrawled a poem, there a lewd drawing, while rusting steel bunkbeds lay piled in a corner. Fading historic photos line the walls; shots of opium poppy fields and military men in ridiculously ornate uniforms, all rotting in the stifling humidity. Many photos of Khun-Sa, always posed just so, reveal a man who thought highly of himself. The room brings to mind my own army days. I can hear the men cursing, sharing stories of home, future dreams and girlfriends far away. Most soldiers fight for God or country but these men fought for narcotics, and who can fault them? Then, as now, it was the single economy of the land; the only way for many to make a living.

The dull daily life of a common soldier, whatever his or her cause, seems unchanged since the first armies were formed.

Heroin poppies have driven the economy of these mountains since at least the early 19th century when the demand for morphine for wounded soldiers of the occupying British army was paramount. More than half of that production went into the illicit trade. Local hill tribes, the Akha, Hmong, and Lahu, grew the plants and harvested them for the highest bidder, be that a drug lord or military officer. The sheer quantity from the area was so vast and profits so immense as to spawn the name still in use today, "The Golden Triangle." This illicit wealth did not trickle down. A handful of drug lords became rich while those at the bottom of the food chain remained trapped in lives of poverty and hard labor.

Walking between buildings, I pass a dew-filled spider web the size of a carpet, back lit by the sun that dazzles like woven diamonds. The spider, golden yellow and larger than my fist, dances across the web like a ballerina to grab a trapped fly as the never ending cycle of life and death plays out in this heavily animist region. People believe their ancestors inhabit their homes and so they make altars to honor them while placing fetishes over doorways to block evil spirits. Over all of this, the spirit of Khun-Sa presides as the ultimate parent figure, a constant in peoples' lives. These mountains are closed to the outside world, forever a part of the distant past where a demagogue can be worshipped.

With no more wars to fight, the Kuomintang assimilated into local life, transitioning from soldiers into "tax collectors," levying a charge on local drug smugglers for crossing their lands, surviving on the dream that their new enterprise would one day fund an invasion force to retake their ancestral homelands to the north. Chang Chi-Fu refused to pay this levy and began open hostilities against the Kuomintang. By 1963 he had expanded his personal army, changed his name to Khun-Sa (Prosperous Prince), and turned on the Burmese government, also taking control of vast mountain areas while expanding the growth, harvesting, and processing of heroin poppies. Other minor thugs joined Khun-Sa under the protection of his personal militia and by 1967 he was challenging the Kuomintang for outright control of the area.

An old lady shuffles under a bent back across the courtyard, carrying a cloth-covered basket. She spits bloody red betel nut juice through rotting teeth and pads along as one saddled with arthritis. With a rusting skeleton key, she opens a massive padlock on a rotting door that I can put my fist through. I enter a square, unpainted, concrete room with a single window that has wooden shutters. Geckos scurry across the ceiling as I enter. It is the austere bedroom of the drug lord himself. There is a small bed, desk and chair, a few personal mementos hang on the wall; a sword, a hat, a walking stick. On a bureau sits a small wash basin under two aging photos, one of Sa in peasant dress, the other of him among his soldiers. There are two plaster busts of Sa next to a can of talcum powder and a plastic wastebasket sits on the floor. The permanence of the room, exactly as he left it, makes me feel that he might walk back in at any moment. It is the kind of room a monk might occupy but not the richest man of his time. Why would someone of unlimited wealth live like this? The old lady has brought food on a plate and a fresh bottle of water that she places in front of a photo of Khun-Sa. She removes the food already sitting there decaying in the heat and bows before the photo with hands clasped under her chin in classical Shan greeting. I realize this is a daily ritual for her. This is not just his former room, but a shrine to a man who has assumed almost deity like status since his death.

After a three-day battle, both Khun-Sa and the Kuomintang were both betrayed by a Laotian air force commander who carpet-bombed the battle sight and made off with most of the heroin, effectively ending Sa's operation. In 1967, he was captured by the Burmese government and languished in prison until 1972 when he was released in a prisoner exchange. His henchmen had kidnapped government officials in order to secure his release. After that, he dropped out of sight, covertly rebuilding his personal army and re-establishing his drug connections. In 1976, he resumed full growing and smuggling operations. During this time, he became the local equivalent of Robin Hood, understanding that the mountain people would protect him if he treated him well.

The lady bows and moves to his bed to smooth a slight rumple in the covering as though caressing a sacred object. She bends to pick up a single leaf I have tracked in on my boots. Her master's clothes still hang against the wall in plastic covers appearing neatly ironed. He did not live like this out of fear. Material comfort meant little to him. Like most of his kind, he was about power. He lived here because he was loved and protected by the people he took care of, the monster as benefactor, a story as old as humanity that has repeated itself elsewhere with the current Cali and Sinaloa cartels.

In 1976, under pressure from the U.S. Drug Enforcement Agency, Khun-Sa moved his operation to a new base inside Thailand in the village of Ban Hin Taek. He renamed his guerillas the Shan United Army and raided local military stations under cover of fighting for Shan autonomy but really to secure more weapons and munitions. Repeated assassination attempts by both the Thai and Burmese government failed, but forced him to move yet again, this time just over the border into Myanmar. None of this stopped or even ebbed the tidal flow of illicit drugs, which at the time were estimated by the DEA to be 70 percent of the entire heroin flowing into the United States.

Local villagers arrive, hearing through the jungle grapevine that a giant outsider from the West has come. They are diminutive people, rising barely to my belt buckle and the women openly laugh at my size. They are the color of saddle leather with the gnarled hands of laborers. These are the people who for at least two centuries have supplied both criminals and hospitals with heroin. They encircle me as both a curiosity and a celebrity. I am a rare distraction from a harsh life. After brief introductions, I follow them into an adjoining room and there before me, sits the man himself. Upon his death, a local artist was commissioned to create a full-sized statue of Khun-Sa. He is made from plaster but meticulously painted so that in low light he appears ready to rise from his chair. On a table before him there is an ashtray with a pack of his favorite cigarettes, one half smoked, and a fresh bottle of water. Behind him is a framed photo of him sitting jauntily on his favored horse, a pistol on his hip. He now sits forever like a Buddha on a throne, in the room where he once gave orders that ended lives.

Like those who followed in his footsteps such as "El Chapo" Guzman and Pablo Escobar, Khun-Sa insulated himself from the arm of the law by lavishing wealth beyond imagination on the local people. A pittance to him was a fortune to the peasants who worked in his poppy fields, but it was enough to win their allegiance and love. In effect, it provided him with a separate army, who directed officials in the opposite direction, warned of raids, and gave him countless hiding places if necessary in local villages. The uneducated people of these mountains probably had no real concept of where their product goes or what it does, either then or now. It was and is simply a way to make a living by doing the bidding of their kindly master.

One by one the people file in, removing their sandals and bowing before the plaster image before them like pilgrims at a shrine. In single file, they circle the statue and beckon me to follow them outside. Several yards away there is a lif- sized statue of Khun-Sa on his horse, another plaster statue rapidly deteriorating in the sun and rain, reduced now to an almost comic representation. Two women approach the statue and lay fresh flowers at the horses' feet. One small child hands me a bouquet to join in but I cannot bring myself to do such honor to this man. I hand the flowers to a tiny girl who places them with solemnity beyond her years.

In 1985, Khun-Sa merged his military force with the local regular Shan army that gave him effective control of the entire region of northern Laos, Thailand, and Burma. From 1976-1994 the U.S Drug Enforcement Administration estimated that 80 percent of all street heroin reaching the United States came from the fields controlled by Khun-Sa and it was 90 percent pure; finer than any other on the market. Combined task forces from four countries constantly combed the jungle in the hunt but he always eluded or bought off his pursuers.

In the shade of a flowering vine, I sit to listen as the people tell me their stories of Khun-Sa. The elders who knew him personally, speak with a reverence hard to comprehend. The almost childlike naiveté of these people allows me to see how they would remember him with such love. Meaning no disrespect, they remind me of a dog that gets kicked by its master and yet returns time and again with nothing but love and admiration proving also that high among their attributes is loyalty. They are simple people, without guile, agenda, or even dreams. For them, life is daily repetitive labor, and when you are born into that, dreams rarely have time to grow. By their actions, these people have turned the story of a man into myth and legend that will only grow larger with each telling.

In 1988, under international pressure, Khun-Sa offered to sell his entire annual crop to the United States and Australia together for a combined price of $50 million, which would effectively eliminate the street market for heroin in both countries, and indirectly amounted to a subsidy for not peddling his product on the open market. Australia turned down the offer saying it did not deal with criminals.

The children sing a song of Khun-Sa's life. The entire day has seemed almost ceremonial and I wonder how often such obeisance is paid to this deceased legend. Was it staged just for me? I did not get that feeling. No one knew I was coming or when. I think I was simply an excuse for a spontaneous outpouring of affection or maybe just a day off from the drudgery of working in the field. Maybe they revere this man because he came from among them or maybe they just need something larger than themselves to get them through.

In 1989, Khun-sa offered yet again to sell his entire crop to the United States for $80 million and was indicted by a New York federal court. Following this, he offered to sell his crop in exchange for $210 million in United Nations assistance, $265 million in foreign investments, and another $90 million for a crop eradication program that would also provide education and health care to the local hill people. This offer was also turned down. In an interview given that year, he claimed his personal army to be 31,000 strong, but fearing extradition under his New York indictment, Khun-Sa fled to Yangon where he surrendered to Burmese authorities but was never arrested.

What is this common historic thread that connects such power-ful criminals? Most were born into poverty and yet blessed with superior intelligence and survival instincts. There is a drive to suc-ceed at all costs, to leave the past behind and raise oneself up regardless of how it is done. But power seems to feed itself, growing unchecked until the actions overwhelm and consume the doer. In the end no one gets out alive and the saddest part is the people who unknowingly enable all of it.

The United States offered a $2 million reward for Khun-Sa's arrest but the Burmese government refused to pros-ecute him and he lived out his days in a comfortable estate fueled by his ill-gotten investments. He died in 2007 and the cause was attributed to diabetes and high blood pres-sure. His burial site is unknown. He left behind eight chil-dren, several of whom are successful business people in Yangon, Burma.

Today, it is locally believed that the Kuomintang still control the heroin trade but it has never reached the levels it enjoyed under Khun-Sa. Afghanistan now produces the bulk of the world's heroin and the DEA estimates that only 30 percent of American consumption comes from the triangle.

One by one the people fade back into the jungle and the old care-taker locks the rooms behind us. I sit with my driver for several minutes taking in all that I have learned. The lush mountains towering above me seem so serene and peaceful. Even the mon-keys have stopped their chatter. Suddenly I smell the sweet burn of a heroin-laced cigarette. "To Khun-Sa" my driver says before taking a long drag. "Move over," I say, before taking the wheel.

The king and I

Of Email
and Kings

ONCE, I WENT TO AFRICA IN SEARCH OF A KING.

I had met more than a few over the years, but there was only that one I ever made an effort to find.

Several kings whose paths I crossed had appropriated the title while being mere chiefs, while others had bought and paid for the moniker. Ask as I might, it was always difficult to get a definitive answer as to what constituted being a chief as opposed to being a king, and it all seemed to come down to being able to get away with what they called themselves.

So that is why Africa has so many kings. Some of them are some self-proclaimed, while others are hereditary, and they cover the spectrum from despot to enlightened ruler, but I had never before deliberately sought one out.

The oral histories of Africa allow for personal interpretation and thus the expansion of the truth, and stories of great men usually carry much embellishment creating a chasm between the myth and the actual person. The stories I had heard of this king could only be called legendary; that he was a shape shifter, assuming the guise of a panther at night to prowl the tribal lands of his people.

Some said he could fly, talk to animals, and was a gifted healer. They also said he was only a boy. Some said this king took the throne at age eleven, wise beyond his years, with worldly insight that far exceeded his isolated existence. Such a story begged to be followed.

Centuries ago, the Kaan or Gaan people (pronounced Goon) depending on who is doing the spelling, migrated from Ghana into what is today the southwestern corner of Burkina Faso in West Africa, settling near the once bustling trade center of Loropini in an area of thick forests that is still pockmarked with gold mines. It is rather lawless to this day and has long been an area whose history is steeped in slavery, and, like its South African cousin, the diamond, Loropini gold has fueled its share of local genocides. Three centuries ago, the black kings of Benin, Burkina, and Togo, routinely rounded up their own people to sell them to white slavers from the new world, and today, indentured servitude is still prevalent in this part of Africa. Because of this, the Gaan people retreated deep into the hinterlands long ago.

They are primarily animists and practitioners of voodoo, an ancient but local religion that permeates the eleven West African nations and remains the official belief system of Benin. The Gaan king is elected from and by members of the royal family, rules for life, and is the keeper of traditional fetishes that are the soul of Gaan beliefs. He is also polygamous; a benefit of wearing the crown.

The Gaan were isolated from much of the world until the 1950s when the first paved roads appeared and photos from that era show them hunting in loincloths with bows and arrows, touched only by minimal white contact. Some neighboring tribes have recently been converted by Christian missionaries, but the Gaan have for the most part, steadfastly remained animists, turning their back on the modern world.

Monsoon-clogged roads forced me to abandon my vehicle miles from my destination, stuck in mud up to the axles, forcing a bushwhack through millet fields dried by a scorching sun that included a close encounter with a puff adder.

Hours and miles passed slowly, but in time I broke through into a clearing, my feet sloshing in the sweat inside my boots. Before me in a cleared field stood seven diminutive stone houses that could have accommodated Disney's dwarfs. They were windowless and had door openings but no doors; each contained a seated clay effigy of a former king, each image inlaid with cowry shell eyes and mouth. Their grey pallor suggested I was viewing mummies that seemed lifelike enough to stand and accost me. I had stumbled onto the voodoo soul of the village, a ritual burial ground holding not the bodies of kings, but their magical essence. It was the Gaan place of ritual and source of the king's power. It was there that he would seek the advice of his ancestors when the mantle of rule grew heavy or when he heeded a call to wander through the spirit world.

I slowly went door to door, communing with a line of monarchs that stretched over 28 lives and centuries in time. One day, an effigy of the 29th and current king will join them. The place was his charge so I knew he was close. I did not linger, because in many tribal areas, violating a burial ground, even a virtual one, is a serious offense. I left an offering of salt, more for the benefit of prying eyes than my own beliefs.

A tiny critter path through the millet was as good an exit as any that I followed for perhaps a hundred yards, passing several animal skulls nailed to trees. It was local gris-gris; voodoo fetishes that repel evil spirits, when suddenly, there before me was a village of mud and straw so perfectly camouflaged as to be part of the forest.

I saw his majesty sitting placidly in a wooden deck chair under a shade tree. He was not a boy, but not yet fully a man either. His ebony skin was flawless and he had long thin fingers that would be at home on a piano keyboard, locked in clenched fists under his chin suggesting deep thought. His long caftan and skullcap did not betray his status, and none of the ostentatious trappings that usually accompany African royalty were in evidence. In fact, he had images of turkeys wearing pilgrim hats on his robe, so the king was cool. He turned to offer a slight smile at my approach, saying in French, "I knew you were coming, Papa." "Papa" is a simple term of respect paid to most white-haired men in Africa and did not originate with Mr. Hemingway. I have earned it.

His majesty's simple phrase alluded to psychic abilities, but I knew countless people had seen me fighting my way through the bush, and no doubt the "jungle telegraph" had alerted him to my arrival. Still, that prophetic announcement added to his mystique of special knowledge while throwing me off balance.

He motioned me to a bench in front of him while a lady approached from a nearby hut. She was dark and stately, dressed in a long elegant Western-style dress and sat at his side with her hand on his shoulder, introducing herself in English as his fourth wife and thus a queen. After our initial meeting, the king spoke directly to me in his native tongue, his black eyes never wavering in their stare, while his wife explained that he was in mourning for the death of one of his three other wives and not in the best of spirits, but his quick smile did not betray any such emotion.

I could not help but notice the hood of an aging Nissan sedan poking out from behind another hut and wondered how such an appliance of the outer world had made its way to this place when my own four-wheel drive sat useless several miles away. I asked about the car, because I could see no signs of a usable road. He replied that it was a gift from his people, as though there are used car lots aplenty in the bush, and I decided not to pursue the subject as there were far more pressing topics to inquire of a king.

Now most of the kings I have met in my travels had an angle. More than a few have cashed in on the proliferation of trekking companies that now seek them out, demanding set amounts of payment, usually so much per head, to give an "audience." They will answer a few questions before a lackey appears announcing that matters of state are calling them away. Some trekking companies have elevated minor chiefs to kingship in exchange for higher payments. I had a wad of bills tucked inside my vest for this occasion, prepared as a loner, to be heavily shaken down, but money was never mentioned.

I spoke with him, through her, of all manner of topics, from African politics to the health of our own families. Our conversation wandered up hill and down dale and survived the passing of hours. His most interesting question to me was about snow, asking what it felt like to be cold, as that was something he had never experienced. He asked about American reality television, saying that he thought all television was real, and when I registered surprise at his even knowing about television, he told me he had watched it in a hotel once during a trip to the big city of Ouagadougou. It also explained why he asked me if all American horses could talk. Still, when he asked how they made people small enough to fit into the box it was a great insight to his literal bushman's thought process.

When I asked his name I was told I would not be able to pronounce it, and that his true name was known only to his people, for such knowledge in the hands of his enemies could harm him. That is voodoo.

The king spoke in broad general terms reminding me of a seasoned politician addressing issues without committing to a specific point, and he often used parables as someone used to educating those of lesser knowledge, but referred to himself in the first person, eschewing the royal "we" so often preferred by self-important people. He had the self-assurance of one trained to be a royal, and I guess he had some formal education. Television aside, I found him to be enlightened on current topics for one who lived in such an isolated place. He possessed a quick wit and eloquence, but in no way struck me as a man of greatness. If he was either a shape shifter or gifted healer I got no sense of either.

He came across as a benign ruler who loved his people and did what he thought best for them and in rural Africa it does not take much for a ruler to qualify as a great man. In a land filled with violent despots, a benevolent king would almost certainly be called great by his people, and in Africa, if you achieve greatness, legends quickly grow around you.

Neither was he a disappointment, as we shared a fascinating conversation through the afternoon. His stare was so unwavering I thought he might peer into my soul as we talked, and I felt under different circumstances, we might even become friends. At one point he reached out and laid his hand on my arm in what I took as a simple gesture of friendship and brotherhood.

Had he invited me to spend the night, I would have accepted, but no such invitation was forthcoming. Then I realized the villagers I had seen when I arrived had all disappeared during our lengthy conversation. It occurred to me only then that I might be unnerving to his people while keeping them from their king's attention and I should not overstay my welcome.

I paid respects to both king and queen, thanked them for their time, and stood to leave when he inquired about my vehicle, and showed great surprise when I told him it was parked miles away in thick mud.

He said he could not allow his guest to walk so far and clapped his hands twice producing a small boy from a nearby hut who approached but would not make eye contact. The king whispered in his ear and the boy took off like a shot into the bush. His majesty informed me that the boy was a runner, sent to spread the word to his people who might have motorbikes to come and find me on the trail and take me back to my vehicle. I thanked him profusely and set out walking in hopes they would find me soon. Within minutes, I heard a terrible noise and turned to see the king's aging sedan, belching smoke and chugging along over the rocky ground that passed for a trail. It looked and sounded like a ghost from a Mad Max movie. Its aging paint was sun faded to almost pure metal and its tires were smooth. I stopped as it pulled alongside me, and there behind the wheel sat his majesty. He flung open the door and motioned for me to get in.

He was smiling broadly, proud to show off his ride, and I took in a panoramic view from the American flag deodorizer on the rear view mirror to the candy wrappers at my feet. I was obviously not this king's first trekker and only then did I think perhaps this was how he intended to shake me down for cash but he never asked for money. Dust covered everything and it smelled rancid. I would bet that critters slept inside at night. The windows, if there were any, would not roll up and there was no door handle on my side. The king was secured by a seatbelt but I had none.

I was not yet settled when the king popped the aging clutch with a neck-snapping jerk. It took a while for the old machine to get rolling, but when it did, his majesty swerved off the road and into the millet. Now for those not familiar with millet fields, they are plowed in neat rows, the furrows allowing water to reach the growing stalks on top of the speed bumps. Logic would have dictated that to drive through such a field you would go with the furrows, but his majesty chose instead to drive perpendicular to them, launching my head into the ceiling with each bump while he visibly enjoyed my suffering; in fact' he began yelling with pure glee.

A Cheshire cat grin covered his face as he drove like a tank commander. I waited to hear the snap of an axle, or crunch of a gas tank being ripped from its mooring. Birds took flight in panic and small creatures ran for their lives. We crashed through the jungle like some great prehistoric beast. In the tall dried fields, the king could not see ten feet in front of us and he was having the time of his life. It took a moment, but I got it.

In the village, surrounded by his people, he was the noble leader, quiet and dignified, but there in the bush, behind the wheel of his car, he could be the young boy that still resided in the man's body. Driving his car was his relief from the prison of rule and I was his excuse. We passed startled villagers, wide eyed and open mouthed, as they watched this strange white intruder bouncing along in the king's car, many of them bowing as we passed, but most were too startled to move. Because of that, I probably, and hopefully, entered their oral history as a story.

The king drove with complete abandon and realizing a moment like that would never come again, I surrendered to the now and joined him in howling at the forest spirits at the top of our lungs. I have never had a wilder or more exhilarating ride.

We eventually broke through into a clearing and saw my vehicle ahead where I had left it, finally coming to a halt with a sliding, dust-scattering, brake-wrenching stop. How we found it with our meandering route is beyond me, but the king knew exactly where he was.

His majesty smiled, gesturing toward my Land Rover as calmly as if asking me to take a seat at lunch.

I set my camera in a tree branch and we took a selfie together and then he reached under his robe to hand me a small slip of paper. It was a Xerox with his photo on it and read, "His Majesty, the 29th King of the Gaan." It also had a cell phone number.

So there, under the broiling African sun, I exchanged business cards with a king who drove like a NASCAR veteran and got back into my own vehicle as he put his sedan into reverse and backed away with all the élan that had brought us there.

I have often thought about that encounter and of the two sides of the person I had found. Many times I thought of calling his cell phone but knew the call would not go through, nor would he remember me even if I could speak his tongue.

A couple years passed and one day I received an e-mail from the king. Where he got his connection from is anybody's guess. Either he had learned impeccable English or it was written by another in his name, but I did not care. I could not believe he had kept my card and was reaching out to contact me. He asked if I had enjoyed the ride so it must have stood out in his mind.

We write to each other every few weeks, not important things, just stuff like what snow feels like and whether horses can talk or not, and he told me his car had died not long after our ride. It seems that now, on special occasions and for ceremonies his people attach it to ropes and pull him along while he steers.

Now at dinner parties, I tell people that I have an African king for a pen pal.

I went to Africa to find a king. I became a story for his village and he became mine.

Halis on a satellite phone in the Sahara

The Sahara
Dialogues

FOR ME, TRAVEL HAS LONG BEEN THE GREAT EQUALIZER.

To voluntarily leave ones comfort zone and enter another culture, especially those more exotic and remote, is an act of courage that helps to define our place in the collective consciousness of man. Common ground is an elusive goal for diverse societies, because we are all separated by the minute nuances that define everyday life for each of us. I buried some of my differences in the sands of the Sahara Desert of Mali.

Tuaregs were, in my mind, the last of the last great nomadic desert clans whose society was open to curious outsiders. At least they were until recently. It was my opportunity, as a white Western Christian, to enter the world of Islam, even if theirs was a watered-down version filtered through desert superstition. Since the early 1990s both government and outside factions have decimated the Tuaregs ranks and driven many into exile, the reasons for which deserve their own retelling at another time. Most recently, an incursion by Al Qaeda has limited the country to all but the most intrepid explorers, and so this is a story of better times gone by.

Tuaregs are a Berber ethnic group that range across several countries in North Africa and claim the Sahara Desert as their ancestral homeland. Each major clan calls their part of that desert by a different name and so, in Africa, it has many. Sahara is a term known only in Western countries. They are called "blue men" not because of their indigo robes and turbans (tagelmoust), but because they employ the ink of sea urchins to create the luminous color that in time, saturates the pores of their skin, rendering it permanently blue. I believe them to be the only Islamic faction in which the men cover their faces and the women do not. They entered written history in the fifth century b.c., when the Greek historian Herodotus called them Canaanites or Garamantes, depending on who is interpreting.

They refer to themselves as Imohag (free people) who are fiercely independent and, while some have moved into cities, those who choose life in the Sahel remain warriors of the first order. For more than two millenniums, the have controlled the Trans-Saharan camel caravans whose gold, salt, and slaves have driven the economy of much of Africa. Their oral histories speak of warfare and foreign invasions. I found my own personal Tuareg, Halis Al Moctar, during an internet search, and was surprised to find that he operated out of an internet café in Timbuktu, running day trips into the local Sahel.

At first, he was taken aback by my request to live with and travel among his people, but he eventually agreed, as intrigued by me as I was of him. Shuttling tourists about did not fit my image of a desert lord, but I was not exactly the day-tripping, camera-toting tourist he was used to either. So, after an epic exchange of e-mails I felt that perhaps I had found my guide, not too war-like and not too citified, a middle of the road Tuareg, if you will. He was my logical shot at entering that society and to make the trip happen, I had to put absolute blind faith in some stranger eventually. Only after we had agreed to travel together did it occur to me that I was voluntarily putting myself under control of Sharia law; me; a white Western Christian infidel, far, far from home.

And so, the self-doubts began. How would these nomadic Muslims react to me, a white Western Christian entering their world? Would I be tolerated? Was this a trap? Kidnapping for ransom was and is a common occupation in that part of the world. I spent a sleepless night crossing the Atlantic thinking "What have I done?"

My model for such a trip was the great English explorer, Sir Richard Burton, who in1853 became the first white man to enter the holy city of Mecca disguised as a wandering mendicant. It helped that he spoke 29 languages and had lived for years as an Arab before his journey. I spoke two languages, neither of which was useful in the Sahara, and was an aging white guy from L.A., but still, Sir Richard was my hero because if he had been discovered, he would have forfeited his life. I had no illusions that my own trip would be even a fraction as dangerous, but what I intended was a bit beyond the norm. It is one thing to visit Timbuktu as a tourist, and quite another to pass oneself off as a desert nomad. By any local standards, I was an infidel and there are many who consider impersonation to be a punishable offense.

Tuaregs rarely venture into a city, so Halis created quite a stir when he met me at the Bamako airport in Mali at 2 a.m. All eyes were on him as he towered over the crowd looking like an indigo batman, standing almost seven feet tall wrapped in his tagelmoust, and he stunned everyone present, I included, by lifting me off my feet with his bear hug greeting. He was not what I expected.

He shouldered my bag as if it were a mere wallet and threw it into the back of a gleaming new Land Rover, prompting me to ask half-jokingly where his camel was. "Second car a camel!" he roared, hitting me on the shoulder hard enough to knock me into the front seat. I relaxed a bit, realizing this man with a dagger in his sash, that I only knew from the internet and who was taking me into a trackless wasteland, had a sense of humor; not that it would make my death any more enjoyable. There was regal bearing in his step and the gold trim on his robes told me he held aristocratic status, but he seemed like a regular guy and the Donald Duck air freshener dangling from the Rover mirror was a nice human touch. We drove into the humid night enveloped by the rush of adventure and the fear, at least for me, of the unknown.

We drove for three days to reach Timbuktu, staying in fleabag hotels where Halis would sleep on the floor with his dagger by his head, always between the door and me, and we talked long into the night. He told me of bandits and brigands where we were going, some his enemies, others his friends, but added that I should have no care about it as even the worst of robbers were afraid of Tuaregs and would never attack one.

His personality was magnetic. He would hold my gaze with deep-set black eyes, and unleash fascinating tirades about all manner of things from philosophy to religion, never seeking the upper hand and always listening to my rebuttals while not judging me. His personal brand of Islam was a conglomerate of archaic Judaism and desert superstition filtered through the beard of Allah. I labeled him a closet liberal.

Storytelling, oral histories, and debates are the heritage and pastime of nomadic peoples, and Halis, by both tradition and disposition, was passionate when engaged in any of them. He talked as much with his hands as words, sometimes moving about to act out a scene and he contorted his face into a new character each time one entered the story. He held me so spellbound at these times; I could fancy him on a stage in front of hundreds of rapt listeners like a turbaned Tony Robbins.

He was worldly in the ways of one who has gained knowledge by reading rather than experience and was at times naïve as a child because of his physical isolation, and yet he made me realize the equality of our lives. When he spoke, he was quick to reach out and touch me in that way so misunderstood by men in the West, but common in the Middle East, a touch that only cemented our friendship, and I never doubted for a moment that should the occasion arise, he would die in my defense. But, would I have the same courage for someone I had just met?

We lived on spaghetti as we drove, that international pasta that is ubiquitous the world over, and we drank beer in restaurants at night. Halis kept his can on the ground and only took quick sips when no one could see him lift his face veil. There was an edge to our conversations; the give and take of small talk was strained as we danced around each other searching for common ground. His hubris aside, there was a natural barrier between our worlds that I needed to overcome. I had to remember how far out of our comfort zones we both were and realized that to this man I was like a visitor from Mars, but the burden was mine as I had sought him out. He had stuck his own neck out at least as far as I had because there were many among his people not so tolerant of outside visitors or those who welcome them. As we reached Timbuktu, and looked out at the low flat sameness of the southern Sahel, he let out a long sigh and I sensed him physically deflating for the first time. He was home, and I acknowledged the effort he had made to bring me there.

For three days he had told me of customs, ceremonies, dos and don'ts and I felt awash in desert culture. He dressed me in his own robes, assuring me of the acceptance of his clan, and when we made our way to the remuda (corral) the merchants of this low brown city of mud came out to bow and murmur "Tuaregs," at our passing, some offering us dried fruits, and all of it giving me a glimpse of the respect the blue men command there in the southern terminus of their domain.

We mounted our camels, hung with pigskin water bags and woven mats, and if his clansmen took notice of this infidel, it was not evident. Blowing sand from the harmattan, the constant, hot, desert wind, erased boundaries between land and sky and turned us into silhouettes as we rode into the empty quarter where time halted centuries ago. That afternoon, in a roaring wind, he started a fire with flint and steel, roasted a chicken with feathers still intact and added a can of tuna for our meal. I spent that first night in the desert wrapped in my robes in the sand, feeling as though I had jumped off a cliff and was just starting to fall but I would be nowhere else.

Our second morning out, a low black line on the horizon grew into a caravan of 400 camels hauling salt from the mines in Mauritania. They were heading south to Timbuktu, and as the stench and dust they raised coated me, it also drew me into their midst. The lead drover, spooked by the sight of a Turareg charging at him, pulled an old muzzle-loading rifle from his saddle scabbard, but Halis intervened in time to keep me from getting my head blown off. I ran like a child between their long rows, running my hands over immense blocks of salt, stroking their hairy backs, searching for words to describe this new world and laughing as more than one camel tried to pee on me. Meanwhile, the drovers laughed at my insane show of emotion.

That night by a low fire, I lay in the sand with those men under a Milky Way that arched over both horizons the same way it did over their forefathers when Christ walked the Earth. There were tales of battle and conquest, and women lost. One by one they told stories of love and hate and myths created out of needs to believe; stories that have grown with each telling, filtered through the memory and mood of each narrator, stories that add the flavor of each additional teller and could only have come from the infinite desert. When my turn came, I recited a short poem drawn from some corner of my childhood that no one understood but that was not important. They applauded and hit me on the arms because I had joined in their ceremony. I was one of them.

Halis explained how they navigate by the shape of a dune or the feel of the wind on their skin and the smell of the air. Tuaregs read the desert the way a Polynesian sailor reads the ocean. They live by knowledge imprinted in their DNA from millenniums of wandering the waste-land. These men, hard as leather and quick to fight, also had an easy way about them most of the time, accepting me without question, simply because their unwritten code demanded hospitality and shelter be given to all pilgrims, even their enemies. All were deferential to Halis who had a natural air of leadership about him that I felt sure had trans-ferred to me as his guest, but still I felt their respect for me as one making a sincere effort to learn about their culture.

Our days were spent in the saddle, Halis leading by instinct as we rode from one camp to another where ritual always took precedence. We would make small talk with the headman, drink several glasses of sugar with some tea in it, and more than once I was offered a young lady for an evening or as a wife, whom Halis would always diplo-matically decline on my behalf. The Western concept of only one wife puzzled and amused them but they never questioned it. At every camp I was just one more pilgrim.

We slept side by side under the stars where Halis told me about his god, who greatly resembled my own, and where differences between Muslim and Christian melted into the sand. He spoke of native superstitions; how the men veil their faces to prevent evil spirits from entering the nose or mouth, and how they destroy a man's yurt upon his death for the same purpose. He told me of great warrior leaders his family had produced and explained that the silver amulet he always wore identified his clan and acted as a passport when traveling. We spoke of family, friends, and obligations, and I discovered his great humor that came forth in the form of a laugh that resounded even in the void of the desert.

My preconceptions fell with each dawn as we found that all of our mutual reservations held no value when confronted by honest conversation and that the only great differences between us were self-manufactured. In our time together, we rode more in silence than we talked because no words were necessary. It was also dawning on me how much of my own material-filled life was also not necessary. Our main dialogue was simply togetherness in the vast wonder that is the African desert and the solitude was not wasted as I pondered my place in the grand cosmic scheme. Halis knew that I understood what he was showing me, and that I would take all of it with me when I left. He had gifted me with a reality beyond my limited imagination and I missed nothing in the long hot days.

Our epic ride had taken us in an immense circle of over 100 miles, through countless lives on the edge of what some call civilization, but a different person arrived back in Timbuktu centuries later than the one who had left it.

After a day in the great library that once rivaled that of Alexandria Egypt, Halis presented me with a silver medallion similar to his own, a medallion that only a Tuareg may wear with impunity. Mine announced to the world that I was from his clan and thus family, no matter where I might be.

He drove me to the airport and would not hug me or say goodbye, as that could bring bad luck. He simply hit me hard on the arm, turned and walked out of the terminal.

As my plane rose into the brown haze of the Malian sky, I watched a large silhouette of a man on the only camel in a car-filled parking lot waving goodbye.

Since that time a faction of Al Qaeda has blown up almost 300 sacred Sufi shrines in Timbuktu. They then turned their illogical wrath on the library, a center of learning that was for centuries one of the finest book depositories in the world. Through friends, I have learned that thousands of manuscripts and ancient parchments from that institution have been safely smuggled out under the robes of refugees, and one now resides in my library, awaiting the day it might return to its home. Currently a tentative peace hovers over the country under the temporary protection of the French Military.

My last contact with Halis was an e-mail from a refugee camp in Burkina Faso. He told me he was on his way to America.

I have not heard from him since.

Markus

Walking with
Markus

THE VIEW FROM MY TENT IS A PANORAMA OF THE GREAT RIFT Valley, the immense rock wall in the distance rising slowly from the highlands of Manyara, and creeping northward to terminate in the massive caldera of Ngorogoro Crater.

The weight of history on this land is a physical presence. Evidence of earliest man keeps revealing itself to archeologists, each find pushing back the count of years that my own ancestors have tread where I now stand. I am less than 30 miles from the last nomadic clans of the Hadzabe, East Africa's Stone Age bushmen, and one of three distinct genetic groups from which all of mankind is descended. The valley before me is literally the cradle of humanity.

The bomas of 300,000 Maasai surround me, filling the Manyara Valley like so many brown mushrooms, and early morning cooking fires layer the valley with a low flat mist pushed down by the lingering cool night air. These are the places that call me, places that lighten a traveler's heart and fill the soul.

A figure walks slowly uphill through the mist, robes billowing wraithlike in the morning chill. It is a Maasai from one of the bomas I drove past late last night. He is alone. This is the time of morning when the boys and young men escort the village cattle out to graze, so I assume by his being here that he is above such menial labors. As he draws near I see that his shuka is a deep magenta and he carries an ebony walking stick that identifies him as an elder, a title of respect rather than age. He walks with the grace of one used to authority. His pace is slow and steady, pole-pole, as they say here. He stops just downwind from my tent and with a broad smile addresses me in Swahili, the lingua franca of east Africa. "Jambo Papa," he says, referring to my white hair. In Africa, I am almost always older than the most ancient man in the village and in this land, age commands respect as it does nowhere else. Papa is a common greeting here for an elder of any race. "I welcome you," he adds in heavily accented English.

I share my morning coffee with him as he squats in front of my tent, in that local way my knees no longer allow me to do. His name is Markus and he emphasizes that it is spelled with a K. It is common in Africa for tribal people to adopt a Western name to eliminate their own from being butchered by English-speaking visitors.

Markus smiles broadly at me over our coffee, showing off the gap where his front tooth has been removed to allow the insertion of small food particles, an aging custom from when lockjaw once decimated his people.

After our coffee, Markus stands and begins to walk slowly up the hill behind my camp; a simple gesture is enough to beckon me. I follow him silently. Above the morning clouds, we reach a flatland full of thorny acacia trees and Markus disappears into a thicket. The interior is a much-used campsite and we sit on a fallen tree trunk to examine the bony remnants of previous hunts. The trunk is notched to show the number of days the Moran (newly initiated warriors) have spent here. It is where they come to eat meat privately, no women allowed, in a sort of testosterone-fueled man-cave in the forest, and it is an honor that Markus has revealed it to me. His pantomime of a hunt soon has me laughing out loud and he lifts his shuka to proudly reveal all the scars that come with being a Maasai warrior.

We continue our walk up the hill. Markus pads silently in his rubber sandals made from old truck tires, the Maasai equivalent of Crocs, until we stand on a steep slope, our necks craning backwards to take in the towering immensity of the largest Baobab tree I have ever seen; its spreading boughs most likely home to hundreds of varied creatures. Numerous small branches have been hammered into the side of the Baobab in an alternating pattern and Markus uses them to begin climbing. Twenty feet above me, he points out a large beehive I would not have noticed without him. Sitting on a massive branch, he tells me how the Maasai trail a small black-and-white bird called a honeyguide that brings them to such trees where they make a torch to smoke the bees out in order to steal the honey, a rare delicacy in these parts.

As we retreat back down the hill, Markus points out a dozen different plants and bushes that provide the Maasai with medicine, meticulously explaining how each is harvested and utilized. He shows me old wounds the plants have healed. There is a grace to his movements, a flow that expresses harmony with his surroundings. The Maasai believe that ancestors watch over them as part of the land and Markus seems an organic part of the whole.

We have walked for over three hours and when we are almost back at my tent he stops and just stands silent, taking in the view. He is smiling, but then he has been smiling all day. I stand next to him and whisper, "Enkai," referring to the Maasai equivalent of a deity that is beyond the comprehension of most Western city dwellers. Enkai encompasses all of nature if I have listened correctly, but a more detailed explanation of the meaning is beyond my abilities and probably beyond understanding by anyone not born a Maasai. "Yes, Enkai," he quietly says with great satisfaction. We stand shoulder to shoulder as the sun disappears behind the great rift wall and I have never known a more intense moment of peace.

Arriving at my tent, I invite him to sit with me for coffee once more but he politely refuses. I extend my hand for a farewell shake and he reaches inside his robe to produce a small gourd, meticulously decorated with beadwork, a hallmark of Maasai culture. The gourd is half the size of a tennis ball and has a cork stopper in the top hole. It is a snuff carrier, one of the only true vices of Maasai men, who seem addicted to it. It is the sort of gift only given to a friend. He places it in my palm and closes my fingers around it. With that he turns to walk back down the hill, disappearing into the mist as mysteriously as he first appeared.

I never asked him why he stopped to see me or why he spent the better part of the day sharing esoteric knowledge with me. Perhaps he was simply curious about this lone traveler in his land, when my kind usually arrives in large groups of safari vehicles with cameras clicking. Perhaps he sensed that I was different and would understand in a way that most visitors never can. I like to think that I do.

If I have learned one important lesson from my travels across Africa, it is that tribal people occupy a separate reality than I do. For them there is no distinction between the material and spiritual worlds, and they move between them with alacrity. Markus gifted me with a taste of both worlds and that is the kind of gift all travelers pray for.

Halis calling to prayer

The Last Muezzin
of Timbuktu

Throughout much of the world, an ethereal call
comes to the ear five times a day. It floats light as birdsong
on the wind; an inviting muse, beckoning the listener to
God. It is the Islamic call to prayer known as the adhan,
and the caller is known as a muezzin. But, to simplify them
as callers is to say that Pavarotti is a singer.

The title comes from the Arabic word "Mu'addin,"
which literally means "prayer caller." The first muezzin,
believed to have been chosen by the prophet himself, was
Bilal ibn Rabah, a 7th-century Abyssinian slave from the
Horn of Africa who is thought to be one of the first seven
converts to Islam.

Because of his beliefs, Bilal ibn Rabah suffered great
torture at the hands of his owner before being bought and
freed by a follower of Muhammed. He accompanied the
prophet in his military campaigns as a sort of aid de camp
and was given the honor of carrying the prophet's spear
into battle. With poetic justice, he ended the life of his
former owner at the battle of Badr in what is modern-day
Saudi Arabia in 624 A.D.

But his finest moment came six years later after Muslim forces captured Mecca in 630 A.D. There, because of his loyalty, strength of character, and fine voice, Bilal ibn Rabah was picked to ascend to the top of the Kaaba, that most sacred of Islamic shrines, to send forth the first public call to prayer, and thus began a tradition that continues to this day.

As with most ancient traditions, the muezzins have collided with the modern world; in many places they are being replaced by digital pre-recorded adhans played through loud speakers. This technology is rapidly spreading, and so it came as a great surprise when I was photographing in the sandy back alleys of Timbuktu, that true human ethereal sound found me and led me to Halis al Bokra.

He was lean as a whippet, dressed in a simple well-worn thobe, his head wrapped in an aging tagelmoust, his sandaled feet the color of saddle leather. His sparse beard hugged his chin line and he had the beady black eyes of a desert fox. And then there was his voice. He would walk a block, stop, and throw his head back, flamboyantly framing his mouth with his hands to send forth such an enchanting sound as to defy its human origin. He was at once a singer and a performer.

I followed his meandering route from a discreet distance, not wishing to be noticed and not wanting the moveable concert to end. When finished, he disappeared through a door at the rear of the Djinguereber Mosque. I wandered past hoping to get a look inside but it was dark, so summoning courage I stuck my head inside and called out a hello.

He had continued on to another part of the mosque, but a quick look around spoke volumes of the man. The room was tiny and spartan: A simple wooden chair occupied a corner, its reed seat eaten through, probably by rodents.

There was no window, only the wooden door with no interior lock; the floor was sand. A low bed was made on a straw mattress, and a small wooden table supported a clay oil lamp. There were matches and candles and of course, a heavily dog-eared copy of the Koran, but surprisingly, there was also a book of poetry by Emily Bronte, out of which stuck a delicate, lace-edged bookmark. I was standing inside the monk-like cell of an intellectual aesthete. I almost opened the poetry book to look for an inscription, but, embarrassed by my intrusion, I turned and left without doing so.

The next morning I awoke to the first adhan and followed it to its source. I crept along walls, keeping to the shadows, but rounding a corner I found myself face to face with Halis al Bokram as he asked in accented English why I was following him. Off guard and embarrassed I relied on my fallback reason for such encounters that has bailed me out so many time in the past. "I wish to learn," I said. "My name is Halis," he replied. "Come to my room this afternoon." Then he added, "You know where it is," deepening my embarrassment.

And so began the first of several conversations during my time in this ancient Malian city, sometimes in his room, with me sitting in the chair with half a seat while he sat on the edge of his bed. I told him of my interest in the role of the muezzin, so, by the light of a single candle he began a discourse on the history of his profession.

Before accurate clocks, gathering large masses of faithful was difficult as was communicating over large distances that it was time to pray, so the first minarets were constructed. Minarets are merely hollow towers topped with the crescent icon of Islam. They accommodate a spiral staircase for the muezzin to ascend to an elevated walkway where his voice can carry across the city. At first, only blind men were considered in order to assure those living below the minarets of their privacy from prying eyes, but that practice ended long ago.

The next morning Halis invited me to walk with him and hooked my arm with his in that natural way so common among Middle-Eastern men but misunderstood by many Westerners. He told me how Bilal had set the bar high for future generations of muezzins, so his successors have always been chosen both for their moral character and pleasant voices and each country has annual competitions to choose the finest ones. As we strode the sandy backways of Timbuktu, Halis explained that there are different tonal modes for the adhan and each muezzin is defined by the mode he occupies—much like an opera singer being a baritone or tenor. It becomes their trademark sound. With that he gave out his call softly to show me what he meant, tempering it with subtle variations that struck me as similar to Tuvan throat singing.

Halis went on to tell me that he walked the streets rather than use pre-recordings because he wanted to keep the role pure, as Bilal had intended it to be. But with no protégé, he feared he would be the last of the street muezzins. "No young men seem interested in such a life anymore, they are of the flesh and not the spirit." Then in a whisper that was also a lament he added, "This is a calling to something higher than ourselves and no one is answering."

On a more personal note I asked why he was not married because as a verger, and not considered to be clergy, that, and having a family was an option. He told me that as a young man he had served in the Foreign Legion and during the insurrection in Chad in 1969 he had witnessed such carnage that he has sworn to God that should he survive, he would devote his life to being a chaste mendicant.

I finally had to ask about the book of poetry with the lace bookmark. With a shy smile he answered, "Well, there was once a girl." After that, I asked no more questions.

On our final day we shared a goodbye embrace and I walked away with that enchanting adhan growing fainter in the distance. It is a sound that will stay with me forever.

I receive an occasional letter from Halis as he has no e-mail. He always includes a quote from a Bronte poem after which he signs off with, "Once there was a girl."

PART SIX

Personal Essays

The author and his guide Geoffrey on the Kilimanjaro trail

Listening to
the Silence

"POLÉ" IS A SWAHILI WORD THAT MEANS "SLOWLY." I FIRST heard it on the lower flank of Kilimanjaro in Kenya, East Africa. It would in time, become one of the most important words in my life.

Although approaching fifty at the time, I still held vestiges of the naiveté of youth that convinces us of our immortality. It had long been my way to charge straight ahead while on the road, taking in all I possibly could in the time allowed, always afraid I would miss something, and counting a trip successful by how many new sites I had visited. I saw no reason to alter that course just because I was climbing to the roof of Africa.

Geoffrey, my stalwart guide, kept urging me to go polé as we passed one trekker after another on the trail, until he gave up trying, lagged behind, and forced me to slacken the pace, but by then the die was cast.

He knew I was angry at him for him holding me back but he just took my gaze and said, "Polé is the only way here." Later at 3 a.m., on a perfect night made for climbing and only 1,000 feet from the 19,341-foot summit (5895 m), I collapsed, spent and frustrated. I lay on my back gazing at more stars than I had ever seen, sucking air like a drowning man and totally defeated in a pursuit for the first time. Geoffrey just picked up my pack and quietly said, "No one climbs the mountain unless the mountain allows it." He believed my arrogance had defeated me and that was a heavy weight as I silently followed him polé down through the scree field, realizing then that ignoring his wisdom had cost me the summit.

It was a long flight back from Africa as I visited memories that lacked detail, a litany of all the places I had visited but could only vaguely recall. I had been looking but not seeing, traveling without ever having been. Travel was my passion but I was only passing through it. Maybe there was something to this polé stuff.

Lessons come to us in the most unexpected ways in the most remote places and it is usually in hindsight that we recognize these moments for what they are. That night on the mountain had shown me that my see-all approach to travel had been preventing me from seeing anything at all, but changing ones nature is easier said than done.

Not long afterward, I was introduced to an elder of the Maasai nation by a mutual friend. The Maasai are an ancient people, nomadic herdsmen with a formidable history as warriors, and Moses had invited me to his village in the rural savannahs of southern Kenya. No sooner had I arrived than my new, slow travel plans went out with the dawn as I was overwhelmed by the color, smells, and sheer noble pageantry that is the everyday life of these people. Where some walk, the Maasai stride, and where others stand, the Maasai pose. I had never witnessed such dignity, poise, or sense of self-worth. The entire village projected a regal but heartfelt air that I could feel wrapped around me like a blanket. My new mantra of polé was left by the wayside as I regressed to my usual self, rushing about with a camera in front of my face; behavior which everyone in

the tiny village found very entertaining. Moses, the headman, took it all in with the bemused look of a kindly
father and then asked me to walk with him.

He was stately in his long red shuka (Maasai robe) and
carried an enormous walking stick I could liken to an
Irish shillelagh, only much larger. It was also his staff of
office. The Maasai have no chiefs, only elders, and Moses,
I found out, was at the top of the food chain, not due
to power or intimidation but because of his kindness
and wisdom. I noticed that Moses's tread made no noise
while I sounded like a buffalo crashing through the brush.
He spoke softly, almost in a whisper and his face held a
perpetual smile as though Leonardo himself had painted
it on. He seemed to float through the landscape as an
organic part of it.

He spoke of his life, growing up with wild animals and
reckoned he was probably close to ten when he first heard
a mechanical sound. He was not just an observer of his
world but understood it in the most primal sense. It was
a different world than mine and I found myself calming
in his presence and realized he was imparting knowledge learned by his people through the centuries. He was
teaching me in his silent way, a way that did not betray the
process. When he too used the word polé, it struck home
with new force.

We walked throughout the day and time did not follow us. Moses was the first person I ever met who truly
lived in the moment and the joy he took from this was in
constant evidence. He saw a ballet in the jump of a fish
and heard an aria in the song of a bird. He pointed out
creatures I never would have spotted and had the Maasai
gift of storytelling, ending each tale with a moral twist.
It took three of his parables before I realized that he was
showing me how to look at the world through the eyes
of a child, the eyes I once looked through but which the

modern world had clouded over with distractions and my own self-importance. Polé was starting to make sense.

Before I left, he pressed a small river pebble into my palm and told me to keep it. He said it had power and I was to think of him whenever I touched it. The power was in his words and soon that pebble became my trigger; a constant reminder of the awe and wonder that is all around me. It was my guide, whispering to me from my pocket that I was surrounded at all times by creatures and events much larger than myself. Most importantly, the pebble was a reminder to stop wasting time.

My travels continued to take me further off the beaten path into more and more remote cultures until I found my attitude shifting from "These poor people" to "These are such happy people." There was no sense of time in these places because life was lived by the cycles of the earth and as my days in such places grew, my internal clock slowed.

Gradual immersion in remote cultures began to alter my world vision until I could imagine it before modern technology and I liked what I saw. By escaping from the trappings of the material world, at least temporarily, I was experiencing the natural world in real time for the first time, and it was a revelation. Moses had told me that when you are quiet, all you hear are the sounds of the earth. As I learned to slow down and listen, the sounds began to emerge. The earth was playing a symphony.

Thanks to people like Geoffrey and Moses, I came to realize the gift I had been given. I was not only privileged to travel through these remote societies but had the ability to write about them. Many of the people I visit have no written language and when they pass their loss will leave a gaping hole in the collective consciousness of mankind. By slowing down and immersing myself in these vanishing cultures, I have been able to share them with the world at large that might otherwise have no knowledge of their existence. My books and articles have given them a voice in some small measure where there was none before and that in turn has enriched my own life beyond measure. I now feel I have true purpose, but had I not learned the meaning of the word polé, I might still be passing through the world with blinders on.

Our lives are an evolutionary process in which we change at a glacial pace, influenced along the way by the unconscious details and nuances of all that surrounds us. Living in an industrial nation my life is by necessity, geared to a faster pace. At home, I am surrounded by media and electronic screens. The sound of an engine is never far away while sirens, helicopter rotors, and ringing telephones are all part of life in the big city that will only become more dependent on technology. But these things do not have to dominate that life. In such surroundings it is more difficult to listen to the silence, but once a pilgrim sets foot on that road, there is no turning back. It took time to learn to appreciate the beauty of a sparrow on a phone line or to listen to the flap of a butterfly wing, but now, my God, I see that there is art and music all around me.

My pebble is there also after all these years. It reminds me to step outside at night and gaze at a full moon rather than a television screen and it whispers of the inherent beauty of a spider's web. It tells me how much I enjoy the chirp of a cricket and the expanding ripples of a rain puddle. One can be awed by the wonders in a grain of sand if you have an open heart.

The natural peace of the world is gradually being pushed aside by manmade distractions, not all of them bad, while others are quite necessary, but that same ancient peace once enjoyed by our ancestors is still accessible. All you have to do is slow down, and listen to the silence. It will come to you.

Choosing which story to write next

Thoughts of a World Traveler

I ENTERED THIS WORLD ABOUT THE SAME TIME AS INTERNA-tional air travel so I include commercial flight under the umbrella term of "baby boomers."

A mere half-century after the Wright brothers first lifted humanity into the sky; the giant clipper ships began their first epic voyages through the seas of the air. The great depression and the Second World War had ended, the bitter taste of austerity and rationing was dissipating, and the common man wanted to bust out and see the world because for the first time ever, he really could.

Journeys that used to require months, if not years, could now be made in days, but it quickly became obvious that pilots who only spoke one language could not communicate with traffic control in a foreign land. Oh to have been there for those first early flights that must have been comparable to the building of the tower of Babel. Keeping armies of translators on the payroll was not practical, so an international conference was convened in the United States in 1954, to decide on a universal language of flight and the world chose English. For that, the French have never forgiven us but *c'est la vie*.

As a little boy, I used to sit in my back yard, head craning upward, looking for those majestic metal birds climbing into the clouds that at the time seemed to me to be pure magic. How could those little specks high up in the sky be full of people? How could something that weighed so much lift off into the air? MAGIC!

I remember my father taking me to Los Angeles International Airport (LAX) in the 1950s where we would stand at the end of their glass observation corridor and watch with awe and wonder as giant silver tubes filled with people rose majestically into the clouds. It was also the early days of television but I preferred going to the airport to watch people fly to and fro to anything I could see on that glass screen. The roar of engines filled the glass corridor as though they came from living beasts and nothing else could feel as powerful.

At the time, it was beyond my comprehension to think of entering such a machine at all, let alone doing so on one side of the world and walking off of it on the other.

Now, decades later, I travel for a living, all over Africa and Asia to gather stories for magazines and that is something the little boy from Los Angeles would never have dreamed of. Now, whenever I am stuck in the quagmire of clearing security those days come back to me. I cannot help but reminisce about the time when air travel was not just simple, but fun. We got paper tickets right from the front counter from a person who made you feel welcome and walked directly to the waiting area without getting undressed, felt up, X-rayed, or videotaped. No one looked inside your bags because no one would even think of carrying something dangerous onto an airplane.

Pilots would stand by the boarding door to personally greet each passenger and welcome them on board. To this small boy, the pilots and stewardesses were like gods from another world, a Hollywood fantasy come to life in 3D and to have them speak to you was like a Papal audience. Attendants were called stewardesses and one particular airline dressed them in a bubble space helmet with go-go boots and miniskirt. Once on board, these "Hostesses" as they were referred to, did a slow-motion strip tease until wearing only a slinky top and skirt. Imagine that happening today.

Smoking was permitted in the front half of the plane and terminated in the middle by a small sign as if that would keep the smoke contained in one place, and those old fabric seats each had a built in ash tray on the back. Stewardess walked the aisles with a tray filled with tobacco products announcing, "Cigars, cigarettes, cigars, cigarettes." If you wanted to meet the pilot or see the cockpit, all you had to do was ask. Food and drinks were free if not very tasty, and little guys like me always got a free set of plastic pilot wings pinned on by a very pretty girl in uniform. Flying used to be cool. But the good old' days aside, I really don't mind the countless security checks and standing in line because I see that as the price of my continuing education. I travel to learn, whether for business or pleasure, and consider the act itself to be the finest classroom on Earth.

I have never tired of seeing new places or meeting new people because all of it is information and knowledge, and the more knowledge we have, the less likely we are to be captives of self-inflicted prejudices. If increased security is the price I pay for that, it is a bargain. The comparison of multiple cultures allows us to pick and choose the very best from all of them while showing ourselves to the rest of the world. Travel allows one to be both teacher and student simultaneously.

Traveling within the comfort of one's home, with information gathered electronically and disseminated on a screen, is a gift of knowledge only recently available to much of the world, but convenience aside, actually venturing into a remote village and walking up to a stranger with outstretched hand is a far more rewarding experience. It is the sights and smells, the tactile reality and nuances of everyday life that when personally experienced, offer insight to the collective consciousness of man.

For me, travel has been the great equalizer, between the reality of the world at large and the consumer-oriented lifestyle of my own country. It has taught me that while a man may be clothed in rags he may still be a poet, a philosopher, or perhaps even one who can truly change the world. Seeing how others live makes me appreciate my own life more, not that it is any better or worse, but simply for its differences.

Travel has humbled me and taught me not to judge because the true essence of a person is often hidden behind skin pigment or wardrobe. It has taught me to expect wisdom from the most unlikely people. While I live in a nice house, I have visited countless people who live in mud shacks and grass huts but have never met anyone who would want to change places with me, nor I with them, because travel has taught me there really is no place like home, wherever that may be.

At a time when violence around the world is making international travel more difficult and sometimes, downright scary, perhaps it is the very act of travel that is necessary to help stop the violence. Travel will never stop wars or keep people from hating, but it will introduce us to our global neighbors, and it is far more difficult to strike a neighbor than a stranger.

But still, that is easier said than done. Over a century and a half ago, Mark Twain wrote, "Travel is fatal to prejudice, bigotry, and narrow-mindedness, and many of our people need it sorely on these accounts. Broad, wholesome, charitable views of men and things cannot be acquired by vegetating in one little corner of the earth all one's life-time. During Twains' own reign, the philosopher George Santayana wrote, "Those who do not learn from history are doomed to repeat it."

After so many years, it would seem we still have a lot to learn.

Layla

Travels
with Layla

THIRTEEN YEARS AGO I FELL IN LOVE WITH A WHITE BALL OF
Labrador fur that came into my life by chance from behind
the bars of a city pound. I knew she would change my life,
but had no idea how she would affect my career.

Straight away she taught me two things; when you
bring a dog into your life, one day it will break your heart,
and the journey that takes you to that point is more than
worth it. Layla journeyed more than most dogs.

I was about to leave a steady job to follow my dream
of being a travel writer, a potentially disastrous idea com-
pounded by adding another mouth to feed and care for
over extended periods that I would be gone, but I never
gave it a second thought. She had me at the first wag.

Layla quickly made the connection between my bags
spread across the bed and my leaving, and was adept at con-
veying her displeasure through body language. She followed
me from drawer to bag with tail tucked and ears down as
I ferried quick-dry underwear and socks, sometimes sitting
in the bag so I could not pack it. Negotiations did me no
good, but she could sometimes be bought off with a peanut
butter cookie long enough for me to finish the job.

When I returned from my trips we would continue the ritual of my spreading the bags' contents across the patio for her to roll in, and revel in the exotic aromas of far-away places mixed with my own travel stench. Soon, her depression at my leaving was more than compensated by our reunions.

From the start, when I sat to write my stories, she would jump on the daybed next to my desk and curl up into a ball where I expected her to sleep most of the day while I worked, but that was rarely the case. She was immediately attentive and I noticed her ears would prick and move about like antennas in rhythm with what I was typing. While I know dogs do not see the same images we do, she always appeared to be watching my computer screen.

Before I realized it, we were having extended conversations about where I had been and what I had seen, her bright eyes zeroed in on me with that curious little skin flap that made her appear slightly cross-eyed. I sensed intelligence in her beyond the norm and soon we were conversing in the nuanced non-verbal language that develops between two intelligent creatures synched in harmony; speaking to and understanding each other as only animals and those who love them can.

I would read what I wrote to her and she would cock her head or wag her tail in dissent or agreement, sometimes offering a verbal "woof" for emphasis. If I totally missed the mark, she would turn her back and begin to clean a paw, a subtle suggestion that I rewrite. Of course she could not understand the essence of what I was saying, but she responded to the tone of my voice, and listening to myself read my own words out loud added clarity and focused me on the topic at hand. Assigning her a voice in this process turned my work into pure joy. She became the vehicle through which I would self-edit and push the story to the next level. She became my muse and most diligent critic. Imposing her reactions into my work made me delve deeper, always telling myself that she thought I could do better. I used her to dig deep in my stories the way she would for a bone.

Friends and colleagues knew of this process and were quick to poke fun at me, asking what Layla had been working on or sending me articles for her opinion, and before long, there was a story about Layla in an international newspaper, and she had written a guest column for a local paper. Both articles brought her fan mail. The first one was a hilarious story about how Layla was the entourage leader of her friend Heidi, a Hollywood canine actor. Friends brought her toys from around the world, and she wore a custom made collar from Africa. She had become an international dog.

Telling her my stories took me back to those places in my mind, where I relived minor details that make a quiet story soar, details that get lost in the larger telling, but are, in themselves, tiny gems of vignettes that separate the mundane from exceptional. Together, we circled the globe, from Africa to Asia, Alaska to South America. She was always there with me in my heart.

During these travels people invariably asked about my family, oftentimes wondering why I would be traveling alone. To many rural tribal people, the thought of leaving one's family unless absolutely necessary is unthinkable. Well, I never felt alone as I always carried a small leather locket with a photo of my wife, Irene, and one of Layla. Wherever I slept that night, the open locket was what I saw in the morning.

Needless to say, my family photos brought me many great stories on the road and the further off the beaten path we traveled, the more the photos became a story for those I was meeting.

In most cases, I simply got a friendly laugh followed by a willingness to open up to this crazy writer with his dog photo, and more than once I found myself surrounded by strangers in a bar for whom a couple of drinks unleashed their own memories of canine friendships. Dog people always understood. Since the first wolf slunk out of the forest and hunkered down next to early man's cave-side fire, there has been an unbreakable bond between man and dog that is unequaled and undefinable. Layla and I had the strongest version of that bond.

Today, I am a travel writer, and I believe much of it is due to that chance encounter in a dog pound so long ago. I am also nursing a broken heart because my friend of thirteen years is gone. Just as it has for me, time and travel took their toll on her. We grew old together, and as old friends do, we spent our final days reminiscing about where we had been. I do not regret a single journey and wish there had been more.

It does not matter if she ever understood a word I said or that she never left our home. She traveled all over the world with me, and she always will.

Until the Next Journey

About the Author

James Michael Dorsey is an award-winning author and explorer who has traveled in 48 countries to visit remote cultures before they vanish.

He has written for Lonely Planet, BBC Travel, *BBC Wildlife, Geographic Expeditions, Panorama,* and is a frequent contributor to United Airlines and *Perceptive Travel.* He has also written for *Colliers, The Christian Science Monitor, Los Angeles Times, Wend, Natural History,* and *GoNomad.* He writes for numerous African magazines, and is a travel consultant to Brown & Hudson of London, and correspondent for Camerapix International of Nairobi.

His last book, *Vanishing Tales from Ancient Trails,* is available from all major booksellers. His stories have appeared in 18 anthologies, including *The Best Travel Writing* (Volumes 10, and 11) from Travelers' Tales, plus the 2016 Lonely Planet Travel Anthology. He has won the grand prize for best travel writing from Solas Awards, *Transitions Abroad,* and *Nowhere Magazine.*

He is a fellow of the Explorers Club and former director of the Adventurers Club.

CPSIA information can be obtained
at www.ICGtesting.com
Printed in the USA
LVOW03s0801010318
568181LV00001B/1/P